The Well-Played Life is an invitation to allow our minds to wander outside the boxes of our own limited understanding, and learn to have fun being God's children. It is a prophetic cry for us to rediscover our ability to enjoy fresh forms of spontaneous expression and unbridled joy. Len makes it very clear how we have forgotten who we are as heirs of the Creator, and how we are to be creative, playful, and have fun! Len's insights are at times intuitive and counterintuitive, and always sensory rich, seeking to feed our all-too-often depleted experience of the abundant life. With wit, wisdom, humor, theological brilliance, and childlike simplicity, Len offers us an invitation to do life differently, perhaps even do life the way God intended.

BISHOP MARK J. CHIRONNA
Church On The Living Edge and Mark Chironna Ministries, Orlando, Florida

One of the problems with many modern Christians is that their conceptions of faith are too boring. They've taken the God who animates fireflies and makes donkeys talk and imprisoned Him in their systematic theologies and rigid formulations. They've reduced the wild ride of faith to a list of pietistic dos and don'ts or a couple of rituals performed one tiny hour each week. In moments like these, I'm thankful for Leonard Sweet. *The Well-Played Life* is an invitation to splash around in the pools of God's grace and let the wind of the Spirit tickle your cheeks. It's a call to open your eyes to the wonders and joy of God all around us. This book will capture your heart, stir your soul, and set you free to recover a life that is as fun as it is faithful.

JONATHAN MERRITT
Author of *Jesus Is Better Than You Imagined*

The "younger" Len Sweet grows, the more playful, sincere, deep, and beautiful his writings become. He never runs out of fresh ideas, metaphors, and stories, as this book shows more than ever. It offers a provocative and life-changing look at work as play—as God meant it to be. After hearing Len share some of these ideas during a recent visit to South Africa, I anxiously awaited the publication of this book. Yet it surpassed my wildest expectations. Len smartly unfolds the good news for First, Second, and Third Agers that God has put us in the world not to judge us, but to enjoy us. Vintage Sweet—surely! Biblical truths in beautiful new language—undoubtedly!

STEPHAN JOUBERT
Extraordinary professor of contemporary ecclesiology, University of the Free State, South Africa; research fellow, Radboud University, the Netherlands

Len Sweet reminds us that we are all children of a loving Father, and as such we are made to play, create, and enjoy this precious gift called life. This is a needed and timely reminder.

NEIL COLE
Author of *Organic Church, Church 3.0, Journeys to Significance,* and *Primal Fire*

The Yoda of wordsmithing and cultural insight has delivered another masterpiece. And what a needed piece— in a world where we simply use people and resources with transactional perspectives, with disregard for soul-making. Thanks, Len, for helping us make the connection between the abundant life and the "play-full" life.

REGGIE MCNEAL
Author of *Get Off Your Donkey!* and other non-bestsellers

THE WELL-PLAYED LIFE

WHY PLEASING GOD DOESN'T HAVE TO BE SUCH HARD WORK

LEONARD SWEET

TYNDALE™
MOMENTUM

An Imprint of
Tyndale House Publishers, Inc.

To David McDonald
a Master Jesus Player

Visit Tyndale online at www.tyndale.com.

Visit Tyndale Momentum online at www.tyndalemomentum.com.

TYNDALE is a registered trademark of Tyndale House Publishers, Inc. *Tyndale Momentum* and the Tyndale Momentum logo are trademarks of Tyndale House Publishers, Inc. Tyndale Momentum is an imprint of Tyndale House Publishers, Inc.

The Well-Played Life: Why Pleasing God Doesn't Have to Be Such Hard Work

Copyright © 2014 by Leonard Sweet. All rights reserved.

Cover texture copyright © Flypaper Textures. All rights reserved. Cover photograph of kite copyright © Hocus Focus Studio/iStock. All rights reserved.

Designed by Mark Anthony Lane II

Published in association with the literary agency of Mark Sweeney & Associates, 28540 Altessa Way, Suite 201, Bonita Springs, FL 34135.

Unless otherwise indicated, Scripture quotations are the author's own paraphrase. Other versions are noted in the back matter.

ISBN 978-1-4143-7362-1 (softcover)

Printed in the United States of America

20	19	18	17	16	15	14
7	6	5	4	3	2	1

Contents

Acknowledgments

GROUCHO MARX once said this to an author: "From the moment I picked up your book until I laid it down, I was convulsed by laughter. Someday I intend reading it."

The fact that I am writing a book on a "play ethic" when I am known for my *work* ethic may strike some as the height of hypocrisy—or, like Groucho, keep them laughing so hard that they never get to reading the book.

I deserve the ridicule. Martin Luther suggested that, in order to overcome one's deficiencies, a good preacher "should be willing to let everyone vex and hack away at him."[1]

Vex and hack away.

I used to believe that the quality of life depended on the quality of our work. This book posits the opposite belief: The quality of life depends on the quality of our *play*. It's time I repented of my workaholic ways. I was wrong. I am open to correction, though criticism is hard to take, especially when it comes from a friend, relative, colleague, acquaintance, or stranger. (Did I leave anyone out?)

This is not the first thing I've gotten wrong in my life, and it won't be the last. For instance, in 1 Corinthians 6:10, where it says in the KJV, NASB, and ESV that "revilers" will not inherit the kingdom of God, I used to mistakenly read "revelers." So, for years, I disdained partying as a waste of time and a squandering of soul. Then one day I reread the passage in a different translation and realized that it spoke not against people who *party* too much (revelers), but against people who *hate* too much (revilers).

I almost turned into a reviler myself, and put this book on a back burner, when someone sent me the following e-mail that started a slow burn inside me:

> I was given a copy of a book entitled *The Map: The Way of All Great Men* by one of the men on my journey looking to start a Men's League. I was reading this book and came across this: "I read a lot of Christian books written by older men. God has given great wisdom to men like Tony Campolo, Leonard Sweet, and Eugene Peterson. But I've noticed something about these men: The older they get, the more feminine their musings become. Their theology gets softer and more pliable. I think I know why."

Older men? Softer? Pliable? Hey, I'm not old; I'm at least two decades younger than . . .

But then I realized that my burn-the-candle-at-both-ends lifestyle, my leave-ashes-not-dust ambitions may have made me appear decades older, not younger, than my biological age.

All of life is being *at* play. At certain times, we need to be *in* play, the body of Christ with one mind in mission. This book is the fruit of testing whether being *in* play and being *at* play might be a distinction without a difference.

I have resisted the taxonomies of play, first introduced in the 1990s by Brian Sutton-Smith, and more recently by Matthew Kaiser.[2] I have also resisted dropping down into many other interesting rabbit holes, thanks partly to the warnings and wisdom of my colleague and fiction coauthor Lori Wagner, whose architectural genius helped me design this book.

My wife, Elizabeth, who has a mind that waits for me to catch up, bucked me up when I felt defeated, even though she kept reminding me that few people have less right to an opinion on this subject than I.

My agent, Mark Sweeney, believed in this book when I didn't, and his wife, Janet, kept me writing—with periodic Barnabas blasts that lifted me up when I, and everyone around me, was suffering Sweet fatigue.

Tyndale Momentum, especially publisher Jan Long Harris and my editor, Dave Lindstedt, who prove that it's still possible to be classic and classy.

Jennifer Tyler was always present to beam fresh light on familiar issues and stories. Kathi Ambler ladled out generous helpings of encouragement and support and was a spiritual gusher of inspiration through her links and pioneering play in the metaverses of SecondLife and SpotOn3D.

My debt-collecting for this book extends to my social media friends on Twitter, Facebook, and Google+, where I periodically test-ran a sentence or thought. Invariably my efforts were enhanced by the contributions of others. This book could not have been written without addenda and corrigenda from my TGIF (Twitter Google Instagram Facebook) collaborators.

The Lord be with you.

And also with you.

Let us play.

Introduction

PLEASING GOD MEANS LIVING IN GOD'S PLEASURE

PLAY BRINGS FAITH TO LIFE. A nineteenth-century immigrant, after passing through Ellis Island by way of the Statue of Liberty, was found walking the tracks of the Lehigh Valley Railroad in New Jersey. On his back and in his arms he carried everything he had brought from the Old Country. Though fatigued and footsore, he shuffled along the rails until an agent stopped him and warned him to get off the tracks lest he be hit by a train or arrested for trespassing.

The man refused, instead producing a railroad ticket good from Jersey City to Scranton. The agent looked at him in shock and asked why he was walking when he could ride. The immigrant said he thought the ticket gave him only the privilege of walking the rails. He almost danced for joy when he learned that he could ride the train instead of trudging the tracks.[1]

"We've got a ticket to ride!" is how the Beatles put the invitation to love and play. One wonders how the heavenly host look at us, slogging along and working our way through life, when we were given free passage to rise, ride, and "mount up on wings as eagles." We were created to be a risen people. Christians are not those who "make life work." We are those who make life fun.

It's time to abolish work. It's time for a theology of play. After five hundred years, the Protestant work ethic has not made us better disciples, only weary and cranky human beings struggling in vain to snag the unattainable dangling carrot we have named "assurance" or being driven forward by the damning stick of "eternity." Whether stick or carrot, the donkey's dilemma is the same.

> *We never know how high we are*
> *Till we are called to rise.*
>
> **EMILY DICKINSON**

Despite reformers such as Luther, Wesley, Hus, and others who emphasized justification by faith alone, we still would rather think of ways of keeping ourselves "in line" rather than keeping ourselves "in love." How can we make the continental shift from finding our assurance not as attainment but as atonement? How can we find the assurance that comes not from "extreme productivity," as one recent book title has it, but from trusting in the veracity of faith and the ferocity of God's love? How can we move from "My life is in my work" to "My life is in my play"?

When I hear people talk about, with an almost pharisaic pride, the merits of hard work and the desire to be better disciples by adhering to laws and labors rather than grace and quiet, it is like chewing on barbed wire. How quickly the language of faith unwinds a toilet roll of talking points about *toiling* at our creativity, *working* at our relationships, *travailing* at our faith, *working* at improving our lives, *working* at living a more God-filled mission.

How did we get so addicted to work? For many of us, we

bought into a form of the Protestant work ethic that taught us that the harder we work and the more successful we become, the more God is pleased and the more we feel the assurance of our salvation. Even Calvinist Marilynne Robinson, in her Pulitzer Prize–winning novel, *Gilead*, shows what a misreading of truth this is. Through her character the Reverend John Ames, Robinson shows how God has placed us on earth not to judge us, but to enjoy us, and that our obligations to our Creator are no less aesthetic than moral. "All things are yours . . . things present or things to come."[2] Or, as Paul told Timothy, God "gives us richly all things to enjoy."[3]

We do our best to make light of our addiction to work, and a whole series of television comedies have explored various aspects of Freud's dictum: "All there is in life that is worth anything is love and work."[4] Beginning with *The Mary Tyler Moore Show*, proceeding with *Seinfeld*, and culminating with *30 Rock* and *The Office*, some of the most popular, memorialized, and award-winning shows on TV have been those that parodied how we worship our work and work at our play. The only "positive" category in which the United States still shows up #1 in the world is . . . who works the hardest and longest. We are a driven people—driven by the market, driven by greed, driven by excellence, driven by ambition, driven by people pleasing, driven by a consumer economy

There are a thousand thousand reasons to live this life, every one of them sufficient. . . . Wherever you turn your eyes the world can shine like transfiguration.

MARILYNNE ROBINSON, *GILEAD*

that demands we work harder and harder to fall less farther behind. Who works the hardest and longest has become a bragging right. Preachers are especially notorious for their BMB (Behold-Me-Busy) syndrome. It's even seen as a virtue to kill ourselves from working so hard.

I have been privileged in my life to be mentored by four giants of the pastoral arts: Fred Yoos of Central Presbyterian Church in Geneseo, New York; Luther Ridgeway of Wesley United Methodist Church in Rochester, New York; Bill Quick of Metropolitan United Methodist Church in Detroit; and Frank Harrington of Peachtree Presbyterian Church in Atlanta.

They were all great pastors, but they all paid the price. Fred Yoos died early from working too hard and trying to please everybody. Luther Ridgeway spent time in a psychiatric hospital from the physical and mental exhaustion of trying to please everybody and working too hard. Though he recovered fully thanks to the therapy of rocks, roses, and a rope of hope named Emma, he died shortly after he retired.[5] Bill Quick is still alive and teaching at Duke Divinity School, but only after multiple heart attacks from a 24/7 work schedule and serving the wider church.

Frank Harrington is a glass case exhibit for this book. Pastor of the largest Presbyterian church in North America, Frank asked me to give one day a year to his 12,000-member church to lead a "staff retreat." He always began the day with a disclaimer: "Well, Sweet's back. I know he's going to make me mad. I know I'm going to disagree with a lot of what he has to say. But I know I need to listen to him, and if *I* need to, *you* need to. So, Leonard, we're yours for the day."

The last time I was there, I could see in Frank's face how weary and worn he'd become. We ate lunch at a diner, which he took over with his all-consuming presence, until finally, after about fifteen minutes of making the rounds, he sat down in our booth. I leaned over the daily specials he'd ordered for both of us, and whispered so no one else would hear, "Your face shouts, 'Time for a sabbatical,' Frank." When he heard this, he visibly perked up, as if I had paid him a compliment, as if looking weary and worn was a badge of honor.

As a historian, I've thought about how workaholism is perhaps our equivalent to consumption (pulmonary tuberculosis), which became the *chic* of Enlightenment culture in the nineteenth century. Called the "white plague," consumption was associated with rich, ambitious, and important people. In our day, has workaholism become a

———————— ◇ ————————

Creativity is intelligence having fun.

ALBERT EINSTEIN

———————————————

"glamorous plague," one that marks its carriers as diamond-level suffering servants, as spiritual and worthy leaders?[6]

A few weeks after the staff retreat, Frank entered the hospital with pneumonia and never left. His body was too weak to fight off the infection. His friends talked in pious, admiring tones about how "Frank's love for his church killed him," and his obituary celebrated what a "hard worker" he was.[7]

Philosophers Jean-Paul Sartre and Albert Camus first met in June 1943, in the lobby at the opening of Sartre's play *The Flies*. It was the beginning of a close friendship and then a colossal fallout. One evening, Camus asked Sartre, "Why are you trying so hard?"[8]

It's a good question. Why are so many of us trying so hard at working so hard when we were created to *play* and enjoy our relationships with God, each other, and creation? It's as if the purveyors of the Protestant work ethic heard Jesus say, "Come unto me all who labor and are heavy laden, and I will give you . . . more work." Protestantism's "divine taskmaster" and Jesus' "gospel of labor," as it came to be called, turned us all into can't-say-no good workers and aristocrats of suffering. They've even cast Jesus as a "working man" who labored for a living. It's almost as if we've taken to heart the sign over the gates at Auschwitz that greeted every victim: *Arbeit Macht Frei* ("Working Makes Free"). It isn't *work* that makes us free. It's *grace* that makes us free.

God is conceived of in many ways (e.g., engineer, lion, computer), but seldom as an artist who loves to play and delights in divine creations. G. K. Chesterton is one of the few who approached God as an artist, understood that Creation was creative, and viewed God as a playwright who had written a good drama messed up by the actors. The universe is not God at work, but God at play.

There is no creation without play. Play is oxygen for the imagination, which sparks creativity, which ignites innovation, which combusts in paradigm shifts. All human creation is recreation. God did not create us to work at life, but to play and find joy in living. When Jesus said, "I have come that you might have life," he didn't then spend his time on earth showing us how to work harder to attain life by our own means; he showed us how much God wants to walk with us in the Garden—or what our ancestors referred to as "walking on the King's highway"—and how playing in our relationships, both divine and human, can make life "joy unspeakable and full of glory."[9]

The art of living is in play, not work. Our bodies are calibrated for the law of gravity, but our souls are calibrated for laws of levity (grace, lightness, play, joy).

I didn't first learn this from Jesus. I learned it from piano lessons. You don't *work* a piano. You *play* a piano.

◇

God . . . is not a mega-manufacturer . . . not a celestial engineer . . . but an artist . . . who made the world . . . simply for the love and delight of it.

TERRY EAGLETON

Mrs. Busick was my earliest piano teacher. She lived only a couple of blocks away on Park Street, but the journey from the ragged upright piano in my house on Bloomingdale Avenue to the majestic grand that greeted me as I entered her front door, and which took up the entire living room of her small duplex, seemed like eons.

I still can remember the seductive kitchen smells that ushered me to my doom at the piano bench, where the judgments of my desultory fingering practices were executed by Mrs. Busick, an imposing woman with a jutting jaw. She would take off her apron as she took up her somber role as a Scribner music instructor who taught the kids who lived on the Hungry Hill side of town. I soon learned that every lesson was preparation for an annual recital, after which Mrs. Busick's students would receive a reward of a small, chalky statue of one composer or another.

Mrs. Busick could be very patient with me for mistakes made in the middle of a piece. But beginnings and endings were another matter. Especially endings, which she expected to be practiced to perfection.

"You can make a mistake in the beginning or in the middle or in some other place along the way. But all will be forgotten when you make the ending glorious."

This is a book about beginnings, middles, and endings that are glorious. But it's not the kind of book that praises the martyrdom of constrictions and restrictions, the masochism of perfectionism, or the rewards of achievement. This is a book about "music appreciation," where beginnings, middles, and endings are all glorious melodies in the ears of God when played for the pleasure of the Lord. Even more, it is a book about the grace notes and improvised flourishes, both resonant and dissonant, that turn an ordinary life into an extraordinary birthright—and a life of work into a life of play.

I had a short life span as a musician, and an even shorter attention span. Mrs. Busick would rebuke me for abandoning a sheet of music when it did not catch my musical fancy. "Finish what you start," she would say with a stern brow. I will never forget the one time she got so frustrated with me over this that she took the money I had brought for the lesson (almost all in coins, as her payments came straight from my piggy bank) and threw it disgustedly on the floor, most of it rolling down into the wrought-iron heating vent (to my unsanctified delight).

"Finish what you start." Today, this phrase rings as words of wisdom in a different sense. How many epitaphs could read, "He lived eighty years, but died forty years ago." So many die intellectually, spiritually, emotionally, years before their physical deaths. The world is filled with the living dead: joyless, passionless, zeal-less, lifeless Christians. The walking dead abound, and deadness is around every corner. Zombie apocalypse is not always apocalyptic. Zombie Christians are walking among us everywhere. The heart can stop living long before it stops beating. And the work ethic that would consume us has put some in the grave far too early.

"I shall not die, but live," the psalmist sings in one of the Passover hymns.[10] Have you decided to live and not die? Edna St. Vincent Millay answered that question with resolve: "I shall die, but that is all that I shall do for Death."[11] Too many are dying years ahead of their deaths. Jesus is not asking us to die for those we love. The issue is less whether we are ready to die for our people than if we are ready to live for them.

> ◇
>
> *Death is not a period that ends the great sentence of life, but a comma that punctuates it to more lofty significance.*
> MARTIN LUTHER KING JR.

When I was growing up, I used to think Christians were people with buns and butch haircuts, wearing dark suits and starched shirts in July, who rarely smiled but waved hankies when they were happy, which was seldom. We have not followed Paul, who instructed us to "never let your zeal flag;

maintain the spiritual glow."[12] Is your glow on? Are you radiating life?

How do we live and not die? How do we grow and glow throughout all of life? What if we approached every moment of life as a banquet of possibilities and a ballet of serendipities? How can we make our lives as disciples a joyful, playful, and passionate experience of the gospel and not a drudgery of duty?

We don't start out with a ponderous outlook on life. When we're young, our world is filled with the joy of play, and by playing we foster our relationships and engage with the world. We first learn to engage with God in the same way. But what happens after that? Why do we change so much? Why does life become so serious, so work-focused, so disillusioned, and so rigid and joyless for so many?

◇

I tell you the truth: Unless you change and become like little children, you will never enter the kingdom of heaven.

JESUS

Why have we associated adult discipleship with Jesus as a solemn, pseudomasochistic affair, when the gospel clearly tells us to be joyful and to "become like little children"? To answer this question, we need to take a closer look at our understanding of what it means to *please* God, and how that understanding changes throughout our lives.

Many of us utter these two words—"please God"—many times a day. Then we add a comma, a bit of punctuation that changes everything. "Please, God!" is a plea for help, for additional assistance; the truth is, we've already been given everything we need to "glorify God and enjoy him forever."[13] The problem is not with God's insufficient supply (hence the comma), but with our inability, or refusal, to receive with joy and praise what we've already been given. We fail to open our hands to be filled with God's bounty because our hands are clasped on other things, or we have confused *pleasing* God with *appeasing* God. But when we engage in our relationship with God with joy and dancing, in *play*, no matter our age, we "please God" by taking pleasure in the gift of life and relationship with the Creator and spreading that joy to others. In God's pleasure, we are blessed, and thus can be a blessing to others.

The Hebrew word translated "to bless" means "to bring a gift to another while kneeling in respect." To be "blessed" by God means to be in a perpetual state both of joyful thankfulness for God's grace that meets us where we are, and of readiness to give of ourselves to others where they are, as we fall on our knees in humble and joyful service before the Lord (as the French carol "O Holy

◇

It is forbidden to become old.
RABBI NACHMAN OF BRESLOV

Night" suggests). In our joyful awareness of our blessings, we replace the comma's "request" to be served by God ("Please, God") with the simple-space desire to serve God instead ("Please God")—that is, to be "pleasing in God's sight," and to "make the Lord's face radiate with joy because of you."[14]

But "service" is not *work*. Our service is not a matter of grudging obligation, not a matter of "attaining" God's pleasure or salvation through our to-do lists. Our service is a matter of joy and the *warming* of our hearts in love. When we engage with God in faith and love, when we engage with the world in faith and love, we live and serve in God's glowing pleasure. We mustn't *work* at giving, but *play* at life so passionately that giving becomes part of the weave of our relationships with God and others.

We become what we spend most of our time doing, and like those with whom we spend the most time. Workers become work. Players become play. Workers become workhorses and workaholics. Players become playwrights and playmakers who write the stories of their lives according to a chosen narrative and then "play" those stories with other players.

A wedding ceremony was about to begin. Members of the bridal procession anxiously waited for the organ music to accompany them down the aisle. But there was only silence. One of the ushers tried to get the organist's attention by snapping his fingers. Still there was silence. The usher then tried clapping his hands. Still no response. Finally, the now panicking usher called out the organist's name. "Neil! . . . Neil!" he shouted, . . . and all the people in the church dropped obediently to their knees.

A "blessed" person is one who falls to his or her knees at the drop of a hate or a hurt. "Blessed are those who have not seen and yet believe."[15] We truly gift God with our lives when we put our lives into God's hands and entrust ourselves to Christ's resurrection presence and promises. To be blessed is to kneel in humility at the sight of human need and in the light of divine grace. Every person we meet is a hurting human being. We don't all hurt in the same places, but we all hurt. Find the hurt and mainline the soul with blessing.

The older we get, the more we need *allowance* and

permission to play, and the more we need instruction on *how* to play. Children play naturally. They can be talked into playing with anyone—even with those from the other end of the playground. Adults line up as mortal enemies. True greatness is the refusal to recognize anyone as an enemy, only as a fellow hurting human being.

When someone tells you, "That's not going to win you any popularity contests," do you begin to launder and lacquer your words to make them acceptable? Or do you say at once, "But I ain't running for office!" Few things are more uncomfortable than a person who is trying too hard to be liked. If our identity is found in Christ, then it matters less and less what people think of us. If our identity is found in experiencing God's pleasure, we don't seek to gather power and popularity for ourselves. If we please God, we're bound to arouse opposition, because pleasing God leads to uncovering the hate, lies, and evil that enslave the world. Every Good Friday is a reminder that we can't side with people who are hurting and not get hurt ourselves. We can't insist on love in a world that hates and not get hated. We can't take up the challenge of change and not get challenged. We can't call for sacrifice and not be sacrificed.

This is what it means to embrace the world in holiness. The concept of holiness is one that Jesus redeemed and redreamed with his ministry. For Jesus, holiness is not a set of rules to adhere to or a group of restrictions to obey. Holiness is not about exclusivity, but inclusivity; about how to be in relationships that exude God's love, rather than excluding God's blessing. An often mistranslated phrase from the Psalms sums up God's blessing of holiness as the joy of the Sabbath feast: "O worship the Lord in the beauty of holiness [or, in His holy courts]. Dance before God all the earth."[16] In Eugene Peterson's translation of the earliest writing in the New Testament (1 Thessalonians 4:1), Paul instructs us to "please God, not in a dogged religious plod, but in a living, spirited dance."[17]

This phrase, "the beauty of holiness," quoted in various ways more than seven times in the Bible, depicts a creation filled with the joy of praising God for life, a world living in harmony of relationships, a world attuned to its Creator.

◇

[Enoch] had this testimony, that he pleased God.

HEBREWS 11:5, KJV

To be human is to be alive in spirit. To be a Christian is to be alive in the spirit of Christ. At birth, every undeveloped soul is given a windfall: the breath of God. To develop the soul is to live a Spirit-breathed life. But with the reception of that gift (breathing in) comes responsibility for that gift (breathing out). That we would be gracious receivers is what brings pleasure to the Giver. What pleases God is that we would become the apple of the Creator's eye—to bear the fruit and bare the image of Christ in everything we are and do. We are not called to *be* the fruit or to *be* the light (Jesus is both). But we are called to bear the fruit and bare the light.

After taking a call in the locker room, a man asked his racquetball partner, who happened to be a minister, for a favor: "Bro, I've got a pastoral situation that maybe you can help me solve. My wife is getting back from visiting her parents in

Ireland for ten days, and she's expecting me to pick her up at the airport. My boss just called and is requiring my presence at a command performance. Is there any way you could help me out and pick her up for me? If I can't be there, I know she'd appreciate someone special."

The minister said: "I'll be glad to pick up your wife, but how will I know what she looks like? I've never seen her before."

"That's easy," the man replied. "When the whole dismal terminal lights up, as if the sun suddenly came from behind the clouds, just find the source of that radiance. That'll be my wife."

I have a name for people who make the world better simply by being in it: *Godplayers*. Wherever they go, they bring with them "something on high," as Van Gogh said of Rembrandt's paintings. Van Gogh wrote to his brother Theo that his goal as a painter was "to paint men or women with that *je ne sais quoi* of the eternal, of which the halo used to be the symbol, and which we try to achieve through the radiance itself, through the vibrancy of our colourations."[18] When in Arles, in 1888, Van Gogh couldn't find that "*je ne sais quoi* of the eternal" in people, he went outside at night to paint the stars.[19] We were created to shine like stars in the heavens, to give off a God-loitered, love-littered radiance that, in its sheer play of light, makes the world better. Can anyone say that about you? About me?

Our lives give off a lovely light when Christ lives there. To be a follower of Jesus is not to hide that light, but to let our lives shed the loveliness of their light in every stage of life's journey, with all the changing seasons, challenging conditions, interrupting detours, roller-coaster kickers. The power of compound faith to move mountains and create new landscapes of hope and love is bestowed not just upon those who "go out" into the world in Jesus' name. It is also given to those who personate the resurrected life of Jesus in every part of their own lives. Disciples of Jesus do not *mimic* Jesus; we *manifest* him. We are *personators* of Christ, not *im*personators. Christ's presence in our lives is more "thereness" than "likeness," more "withness" than "whatness." Jesus made our creation in the *imago Dei* more "spit" than "image" (as in "spit 'n' image").[20]

Jesus intended for his church to be a communion of the baptized, not a power structure or power struggle of bureaucrats. We've become a most worldly church. To live in God's pleasure is not to wield categories of power for power's sake. It is to know that the healing power of Shalom resides in us with the simple prayer of "Please God." Weakness is the primary strategy of the Cross. How did Christ conquer death and disarm the devil? How did Christ overcome the "powers" and "principalities" of the world? Through (apparent) weakness. "Having disarmed the powers and authorities, he made a public spectacle of them, triumphing over them by the cross."[21] In weakness are all things possible. In Emmanuel, the world can be healed; in Shalom, the world will find peace.

Disciples do not simply seek to "please God" in every decision. God's pleasure is not something we earn, but something we receive as a gift. Disciples of Jesus luxuriate in God's pleasure, and live in such a way that living in God's pleasure becomes second nature, even the very definition of holiness. Fear of pleasure is a sign of depression and lack of aesthetics.

The pleasure phobia of many Christians mirrors the depressed and ugly state of the church. In fact, there are some divine purposes that can be achieved only through pleasure. That's why God created artists.[22]

We know that to please God is the *unum necessarium* . . . the one thing we were created for. But what does it mean to please God in the nitty-gritty of life? How do we find that kind of joy in holiness? And how does that change from when we are five to when we are fifty-five? What does our discipleship look like in the various times of our lives? The need to make discipleship a lifelong mission of living in God's pleasure requires a reframing of what it means to be "pleasing to God" in every age. To please God is not a goal to be attained or an achievement to be sought. It is the relational awareness of joyfully and faithfully living a Sabbath life clothed

———————— ◇ ————————

Every art contributes to the greatest art of all, the art of living.

BERTOLT BRECHT

in God's glory. The Lord's Day is the Lord's way—to relish the freedom to dig in the dirt, explore uncharted territories, hike the highest mountains, and spelunk the deepest caverns of our faith and our world—to go outside and play, missionally and relationally, knowing we live in God's protection and favor. To bask in the pleasure of God is to rediscover and relive the Garden story of strolling with God through paradise, yoked in a covenant relationship that clothes us in God's seamless robe of mercy and grace.

The word most often translated "paradise" in English versions of the Bible actually means "garden." It is the garden walk from which we come, and the garden walk toward which we go. Playing with God in the Garden is the ultimate metaphor for discipleship. Already in the Garden, God strolls among humanity in the morning dew and evening cool, at dawn and at dusk. To please God is to "go outside," to go out and into the world to play in God's presence, according to God's playbook.[23]

To please God, to be pleasing *to* God, is to "walk with Light," to walk with God in joy, praise, holiness, and humility as image-bearers of the Light.

To experience divine pleasure is not to work at life, but to play at life, to walk daily in the Garden radiance of God's pleasure. The greatest compliment paid to anyone in the Bible is the one paid to Enoch: "He walked faithfully with God."[24] We know only this one characteristic of his life, but it was so pleasing to God that it got Enoch what only one other person in the Bible (Elijah) got—a get-out-of-death-free pass.

> *Play can be faithful and faith can be playful.*
>
> LIZ LYNN PERRAUD

Enoch's walk is a walk available to every one of us. It's a walk of *relationship*—with all the complexities that implies; a relationship like that of the prophet Jeremiah, who, in one of the most astonishing passages of Scripture, says, "You are righteous, O Lord, and I cannot disagree with you, yet let me talk with you of your judgments."[25] In other words, God is right (by definition), but our relationship with God entitles us to disagree and to argue with God about our disagreements.

That level of intimacy is rooted in the garden walk. There is a world of difference between those who talk about "The Man Upstairs" and those who can say, "I walked and talked with God this morning."

Bishop James K. Mathews began his ministry in the Methodist church as a missionary in India, where he met Eunice Jones, the daughter of E. Stanley Jones, whom some have called the greatest missionary since St. Paul. Bishop Mathews and Eunice were married for seventy years, and he became a confidant of his father-in-law. When Stanley Jones died in India in 1973, Bishop Mathews was asked if anyone was with him at the end. He replied, "When last seen, Stanley was walking with God, and then God took him."[26]

> *By faith Enoch was taken from this life, so that he did not experience death; . . . before he was taken, he was commended as one who pleased God.*
> HEBREWS 11:5

I call the walk with God the "Great Walk." The Great Walk is not a walk to work. It's a walk in the park, a march to Zion, a walk on the wild side. In the words of G. K. Chesterton, "The more I considered Christianity, the more I found that while it had established a rule and order, the chief aim of that order was to give room for good things to run wild."[27]

The Great Walk is a dance to the "music of the spheres." Teresa of Avila, a designated "doctor of the church," refused to refer to disciples as "working for God" or being "used by God." She deemed those words inappropriate and presumptive. Teresa's preferred metaphor for walking with God was "casting flowers," as children cast flowers to the crowds in a parade. Our mission in life, she said, is to "cast flowers" before God, and in so doing, "to give pleasure to Jesus."[28]

How do we engage with God in a way that is pleasing to our Creator? How do we "walk with God" in the garden? I like to call it Godplay. This book is about how to engage in Godplay in every age of life.

Living a "well-played" life means experiencing the fullness of joy that comes from being in deep with the divine, cleaving close to the covenant, living in sync with the Spirit, and yoked to Christ to the point of surrendered trust in God's providences and promises. As in the case of Israel, God's choice of us as "God's people" precedes any obedience on our part. But out of our relational joy in loving God, we find ourselves obedient.

> ◇
>
> *You received from us how you ought to walk and to please God.*
>
> PAUL THE APOSTLE

To engage with God in Godplay is to keep the covenant healthy and holy, which is the secret sauce of happiness. Godplay doesn't wield the power of celebrity or strive to become a "winner" or "star" or "champion." Godplay is not to "win with Jesus" or even to "be somebody with Jesus." Godplay is to pick up a cross, which is more blessing than burden, and follow Jesus.[29] The recipe for a happy life is one that doesn't make happiness paramount, but playfulness.

The Holy Spirit is the presence of Godplay in the world. The Holy Spirit is what turns the Bible from words on a page to the very voice of God speaking. God's Spirit is not "at work" in the world or the Bible. God's Spirit is "at play" in the world and the Bible. The Spirit's playful presence, reveling in God's "very good" of Creation, is found in art, music, liturgy, literature . . . all of which tune our hearts to sing God's praise. Evangelism is playing the music of Jesus, helping others to hear and claim the music playing inside them, and inviting others to play and sing together. Or as Kiki Dee once put it, "I've Got the Music in Me."

If humanity needed Protestantism to show it how to *work*, humanity now needs Godplay to teach it how to play. Godplay restores Jesus' original words, "Come unto me, you who are weary and burdened, and I will give you . . . refreshment."[30] We now know that Jesus himself was less a "working man" than an artisan (*tekton*) who created by artistic means. Perhaps the production of a perfect furrow in a plowed field, or the setting of a flat row of stones before placing the next course, is an artistic achievement.

Godplay is a fundamental approach to life, based not on work and worry but on the biblical warranty that a loving reality called God is inviting us to skip and dance all the way home. The march to Zion is not unremitting toil and travail, but a dance of Shabbat and Shalom by which we "enter into the joy of your lord."[31]

The time is *now* for "good soldiers of Jesus Christ" to desert as "soldiers in the army of the upright,"[32] where the only way we can keep pace in our daily march to the battles of the workplace is through amphetamines, antidepressants, antacids, alcohol, acetaminophen, and so forth. God did not put us here to sacrifice at the altars of a deranged marketism, to earn/

turn in taxes/and burn, to pour out our lives on assignments into which we cannot pour out our hearts. God did not put us here to work like beavers. God put us here to play like otters.

Christians don't work toward the pleasure and acceptance of God. We live from it and play in it. Anytime we approach life with the joy of a child, it is Godplay. Anytime we praise and worship God, it is Godplay. Anytime missional living ramifies relationally in an incarnational way, it is Godplay. The sync of a missional, relational, and incarnational life brings instantaneous and spontaneous joy: Godplay.[33] The world doesn't need more work and more workers, but more play, more God, more Godplay and Godplayers.

What does Godplay look like? How do we become more attuned to playing with God? Godplay lasts a lifetime but can look different at different times in our lives. How we engage in Godplay depends in part on our "age." Not our physical age—though our physical age also suggests different forms of play—but our discipleship "age," which brings to the fore not only age-related behaviors but age-important questions about play and how we play out our lives with God and others.

———— ◇ ————

If work really were such a good thing, then the rich would surely have found a way to keep it for themselves.

HAITIAN PROVERB

Humans are not without resources for dividing life into periods and cycles. The most enduring, perhaps, are the generational divisions. Aboriginal peoples made decisions based on a "seven generation" rule: Project the impact of an action on the seventh generation and decide accordingly. The longevity revolution has complicated the seven generation rule because it might soon be possible to have almost seven generations living side by side.

The psalmist thought in generational terms as well: "God's faithfulness endures from generation to generation."[34] Notice he did not carve up life "from decade to decade" or "from century to century" or "from childhood to adolescence to adulthood." In fact, we don't have the word *teenager* in the English lexicon until 1673, and "decades of life" distinctions don't appear until the last third of the nineteenth century.[35]

In 2002, the president of Turkmenistan issued an edict that divided life into nine twelve-year cycles. Saparmurat Niyazov's decree, published in the national newspaper, *Neutral Turkmenistan*, ended childhood at twelve and extended adolescence to twenty-five. Turkmen "youth," he ruled, will henceforth be between twenty-five and thirty-seven, while those between thirty-seven and forty-nine are "mature." The next twelve-year cycles are labeled *prophetic, inspirational,* and *wise.* Old age begins at eighty-five, while Turkmen who reach age ninety-seven enter a period named for Oguz Khan, considered the founder of the Turkmen nation, who died at 109. Widely mocked after it was first announced, and as arbitrary as the wind blows, this periodization may have been one of the most creative and relevant approaches to aging ever broached.

I have argued elsewhere that, after the boomer generation, generational cultures analysis no longer works in a world where change is exponential, not incremental.[36] But we need some way of talking about the human life cycle. Next oldest to the generational cultures division of humanity is the "ages of man" thinking, which divides the course of life into three, four, six, and seven stages.[37] Psychologists typically divide life into five seasons: infancy, childhood, early adulthood, middle adulthood, and late adulthood.

In recent decades, however, new interest in the phenomenon of delayed aging and a longer life span has revolutionized the way we think about our lives. Cambridge demographic historian and sociologist Peter Laslett argues for four "ages" of life based on four sets of life questions.[38] In the first age, the age of preparation, the questions are, "What will I learn?" "Who am I?" "How will I fit into the world?" In the second age, the age of achievement and acquisition, the questions are, "What will I achieve in the external world?" "What is my identity?" "What is my purpose?" The questions of the third age, the age of self-fulfillment, are, "What makes me happy?" "How can I fulfill myself?" "How do I self-actualize myself in my life?" "How do I grow to my full potential?" The fourth age, or the age of completion, is a time of entering fully into the stage of life that descends into a well-prepared death.[39] British business guru Charles Handy, from the London Business School, presents these four ages as well in using human resources to maximize the political and economic challenges of society.[40]

Long before Laslett and Handy, a Black Forest wood-carver from Brienz, named Johann Huggler, carved a sculpture called "The Three Ages of Man" that some say is his greatest masterpiece. Unlike Titian's "Three Ages of Man," in which the Third Ager is shown hunched over holding skulls and contemplating death, Huggler's Third Ager is vital and moving.

In establishing a framework for our understanding of Godplay, at first I re-architected the way we live into three ages, similar to Peter Laslett's first three.

———————————— ◇ ————————————

I realized that all the experiences I have had—as daughter, student, youthful radical, reporter, battler for women's rights, wife, mother, grandmother, teacher, leader, friend, and lover, confronting real and phantom enemies and dangers, the terrors of divorce and my own denial of age—all of it, mistakes, triumphs, battles lost and won, and moments of despair and exultation, is part of me now. I am myself at this age. *It took me all these years to put the missing pieces together, to confront my own age in terms of integrity and generativity, moving into the unknown future with a comfort now, instead of being stuck in the past. I have never felt so free.*

BETTY FRIEDAN

The question of the First Age (0–30) is "Where do you go to school?" We are now told that, for males, twenty-six—not eighteen—is the new age of "adulthood." But remember: Not that long ago, during the Second World War, twenty-year-old pilots flew the planes that won the war; it was twenty-year-olds whom we entrusted with our best technology to battle the German night fighters. Our parents and grandparents saved the world at the same age today's college students are saving beer cans.

The question of the Second Age (30–60) is, "Where do

you work?" or "What do you do for a living?" In this configuration, these "middle years" are the most fulfilling years of one's life. Carol Shields, the Pulitzer Prize–winning Canadian novelist, put this view succinctly: "There might not be happy endings. . . . I believe in happy middles."[41]

The question of the Third Age (60–90) is, "Where did you retire?" The wellness of the first two ages devolves into the worseness of the last age.

This book argues that, for the Christian disciple engaging in Godplay, the questions for those ages change dramatically from the demographic ones.[42]

In the First Age of life (0–30), the questions are, "How do I learn to live in God's pleasure?" and "How do I learn to play in my relationship with God?"

In the Second Age of life (30–60), the questions become, "How can I retain or regain my sense of play amidst the complexities of my life?" "How can my relationship with God help me find joy in my relationships with family, church, community, and creation?" "How can I become a 'real' player in a culture of FEAR (false expectations and assumptions of what's real)?"

In the Third Age of life (60–90), the questions become, "How can I become a master player and world changer?" "How can I be a coach to others in Godplay?" "How can I be a healing presence for Christ in the world?" Third Agers are not called to save the world. But Third Agers are called to show the world the way in which it can be saved.

These "ages" are not meant to pose sequential and consecutive questions, but simultaneous and concurrent ones.

With each of these God-pleasing ages, the life cycles are not necessarily consecutive but cumulative, and they are more simultaneous than sequential. You can have a 1947 model body and be thirty physically, one hundred intellectually, and three spiritually. In other words, preparedness and practicing are not limited to the First Age.

If we ever graduate from the First Age, we stop listening and learning how to toy and tinker and to think like a child. If we ever graduate from the Second Age, we stop living out the gospel in "real time." If we ever graduate from the Third Age, we stop living in the anointing of mission, in season and out. Ideally, though, we would take the core of each age into the next age and not stop listening and learning and tinkering, living out the gospel, and living in our anointing.

Unlike Laslett and Handy, I end my discussion at the Third Age. Godplayers continue their pilgrimage in sanctification until glorification, the moment of our physical death.

A pilgrimage, by definition, is a journey of transformation; we are never the same at the end as we were at the beginning. For Third Age pilgrims, there is no "retirement," no "age of completion," only excitement for every moment of the future, both during this life and in the next. After all, once God has called us into ministry, does God ever call us out of it? Do we retire from the covenant we entered into? Do we retire from marriage? Billy Graham is famous for saying, "Name me someone in the Bible who 'retired.'" In the words of the apostle Paul, "The gifts and the calling of God are irrevocable."[43]

The gift of increased longevity represents a big and permanent shift in human life—one that may require a new way of thinking about the course of our lives. A productive Third Age is still a very new concept in our society. It is definitely a new concept in the church, a designation that we've never before had to think about the way we do now. But I believe that a new view of aging has the potential to profoundly change the church and change the world.

In the past, for many people, the question of the Third Age has been, "Where did you retire?" or "Where are your golf clubs?" We used to think of the "Third Age" as the age of "retirement," the comparatively brief period of time between work and death, wherein, if we're lucky, we can still travel a bit; enjoy sitting on the porch watching the world go by; and maybe do a few things we've always wanted to do—such as play with the grandchildren—before illness sets in and our lives revolve around doctors' offices and hospital visits.

In fact, throughout most of human history, a "third age" was set aside for only the fortunate few. In the second half of the twentieth century, many USAmericans began to do everything possible to store up funds that would allow them to "retire early"—meaning at fifty-five or sixty, instead of the usual sixty-five. Thanks to revolutionary advances in health care, medical technology, pharmaceuticals, genetics, wellness programs, organic foods, nanotechnology, and robotics, to name but a few, it has now become possible, in the twenty-first century, to enjoy an almost Methusalean life span.

———— ◇ ————

They want somebody to tell 'em they have a chance at the i-n-g of life and not just the e-d.

TOM ROBBINS, *JITTERBUG PERFUME*

Perhaps we should speak of the "younging" of our churches more than their "aging." We now have a Third Age spanning as many years as or more than the first two-thirds of most of history. When we covenant in baptism to "walk with God" as twenty-first-century disciples, for example, we are making an eternal commitment with century-long legs (ditto our til-death-do-us-part marriage partners).

We suddenly find ourselves reeling from the realization that the new Third Age is not a mere five years or so, but possibly thirty, forty, or fifty-plus years. So what do we do with that Third Age when those years might become the best years of our lives? When rock star Elton John was asked what growing older meant to him, he spoke for most aging boomers when he replied, "I still want to make music, but I don't want to look like Donald Duck while I'm doing it."[44] What should disciples of Christ do with an entirely new third-of-life span?

Nothing stinks up the heavens and shuts down the church quite like indolence. *Sloth* is any time or any age when Christians settle into a state of soul in which they expect to live the remainder of their days just about where they are now, doing what they're now doing, without going beyond their present experience and the possibility of any dramatic changes or growth spurts. When a soul lives off the faded splendors of the past, it is sinking into itself and not rising to God's occasions.

Have you considered the possibilities? Has the church? The question now at age sixty is not, "Where should I start on my bucket list?" or, "How do I best set things in order?" or, "Where do I rock?" but, "What should I do with the best years of my life?" "How can my life be pleasing to God during this

Third Age?" "How can I live in God's grace and pleasure?" "How can I honor this unexpected gift?" "What does Godplay mean in terms of eighty to one-hundred-plus years of life?"

An expanding life span requires a fresh way of looking at what it means to live within the pleasure of God and drink deeply of God's well of pleasure.

If you have kids, do you think of them as twenty-second-century children? Apart from my mother, Mabel Boggs Sweet, the person who had the greatest influence on me was Dayton environmentalist, philanthropist, and gardener Marie Aull, whose life span touched three centuries. Marie was born in the nineteenth century (1897) and died in the twenty-first century (2002). Our twenty-second-century kids, who were born in the 1990s or later, stand a good chance, statistically, of living well into the 2100s—"Lord willing, Jesus tarrying, creek not rising, Moses not prohibiting," as my Appalachian gramma used to say.

———— ◇ ————

God is in the bits and pieces of Everyday—
a kiss here and a laugh again, and
sometimes tears.

PATRICK KAVANAGH, "THE GREAT HUNGER"

This dramatic expansion of life span has been relatively recent. Whereas in the 1890s, the average life expectancy for a male was thirty-seven, by the 1990s it had doubled, and now it's even higher, into the mid-eighties. Research published in the 2013 edition of the *Proceedings of the National Academy of Sciences* proposes that, in terms of demographic equivalency, seventy-two is the new thirty.[45] Tell someone in their forties today that they're in "middle age" and you're likely to get smacked in the face.[46]

England's royal family has a tradition of sending out birthday greetings when subjects reach one hundred. In 1916, King George V sent out seventeen. Queen Elizabeth II sent out 255 telegrams in 1952. In 1996, that number was 5,281. In 2007, the number of cards sent was 8,439. In fact, in 2007, 770 people received messages for 105th birthdays and above. The fastest growing segment of the US population percentage-wise are centenarians (one hundred-plus), who are now so numerous, there is a debate among gerontologists as to whether a new category of "super-centenarians" should be created for those over 105, or over 110. Fifty percent of all baby boomers (those born between 1945 and 1972) will live healthy lives beyond one hundred, which has enormous economic consequences since this is the "pig-in-the-python" population that plummeted two centuries of hard work, high accomplishment, and heavy sacrifice into a sinkhole of debt in less than two decades.[47]

If you are reading this in your forties or fifties, you'd be in your dotage if you lived one hundred years ago, when old age was the privilege of wine and cheese. Today, those of you who are forty-five or fifty can expect to keep blowing out birthday candles for another forty years, with a less hardy body but still hale. Thirty-five million USAmericans are now over age sixty-five; in thirty years, that number will double to seventy million.[48] In 1982, the average age of an

———— ◇ ————

Be yourself; everyone else is already taken.

OSCAR WILDE

elderly person entering a nursing home was sixty-five. Today that age is eighty-three. More than half of those between sixty-five and seventy-four think of themselves as "middle-aged" or "young," as do a third of those over seventy-five.[49] When the words are changed to "midlife" or "mid-youth," the numbers go even higher. No doubt about it: People are living "younger" longer.

It is astonishing that most scholars have not applied the discipline of historical context to the first century in this respect. We've been led to think anachronistically of a thirty-year-old Jesus as a "young and fearless prophet."[50] In fact, Jesus' world-changing ministry took place in the first-century equivalent of our Third Age. A more accurate anachronism (if there is such a thing) would be this: In first-century Palestine, First Agers were from one to twelve years old; Second Agers were twelve to thirty; Third Agers were thirty to forty-plus. Life expectancy for males varied from twenty-six (at birth) to fortyish (if you lived to the age of five). In ancient Rome, less than 5 percent of the population survived past sixty.[51] In sum, it's not true that almost no one survived to "old age" until the recent past. But people aged earlier, and were "older" longer.

The honoring of an "ancient of days" and "elder sage" in Jewish circles started at age forty, but you were not "aged" enough to take on disciples, or "seasoned" enough to start teaching, until you reached the ripe age of thirty, the precise age at which Jesus launched his peripatetic seminary.

Although we don't know much about his youth, we do know that Jesus spent his First Age years engaged in learning about God, his Father. In his Second Age, we suspect, he spent his time preparing for his "real" mission and practicing both his scriptural prowess and his craft as a builder or *tekton* (a craftsman, perhaps, of both buildings *and* parables). And in three dynamic Third Age years, Jesus made the greatest mark on the world of anyone in history.

At thirty, Jesus was in the prime of his life. But "prime" meant something closer to our sixty than our thirty. In other words, when Jesus was the equivalent of our "retirement age," he set out on a journey to save the world.

As massive numbers of baby boomers age into an expansive and explosive Third Age, the need for some theological reflection rises to the fore: How can we make the most of this new third-plus of our lives stretching out before us? How can this Third Age be a time when we rock the planet and not just rock on the porch? How can our Third Age years of highest creativity and activity be meaningful and significant? Some studies have shown that human creativity doesn't plateau until age eighty-three, when it begins to level off and then slope downward. Other surveys indicate that happiness peaks at eighty-five—in other words, you get happier and happier the older you get. So much for old age as "the unhappy hour." The Third Age is life's true "happy hour"—the perfect age somewhere between old enough to know better and young enough not to care.

The Third Age challenges us to rethink John Donne's image of old age as lowering our sails as we drift into harbor. The new Third Age is not a struggle to find meaning in our lives amid the frost and blight of winter, but a thrilling challenge to find ways to use the tremendous energy, acumen, and time stretching before us in creative and free ways that feel like play and fun!

But reimagining the Third Age is not just a Third Age question. Nor is it simply a personal and individual question. It is a key question for everyone in this handover from the twentieth century to the twenty-first century, and this handover from a Gutenberg Christianity to a TGIF (Twitter Google Instagram Facebook) Christianity.

What can this transition mean for twenty-first-century discipleship? How can our lives be most pleasing to God in every life cycle, from first cry to last breath? How can we take a fresh look at what this extra time might mean in terms of an entire life span of living in and at the pleasure of God? How can we make our lives playful and joyful while in a missional mode? In fact, what does "taking the gospel into the world," or as I like to reframe it, "joining Jesus in what he's already doing,"[52] look like in a first, second, and third age? While answering these questions, we need to keep as the primary focus of each phase of life the witness and "withness"[53] of Jesus, the one who can show us how to live a life of abundance and abidance "pleasing" to God. Jesus elaborated a theology of abundance, an abundance not measured in dollars and cents but in the deepest hungers of the human heart.

In every age of life, what is your "saving grace" that allows

◇

I will praise You, for I am fearfully and wonderfully made;

Marvelous are Your works,

And that my soul knows very well.

PSALM 139:14-15, NKJV

you to be in mission with Christ—to engage in Godplay as a learner, a real player, a master player, and a game changer in a difficult and dangerous world?

What are our Third Agers doing to join Jesus in saving the world? What are all Agers doing to prepare disciples to reach this level of maturity in fire-breathing, Pentecostal faith in Christ? What is being done to empower and encourage all Agers to mentor others in how to *be* beauty, truth, and goodness in person? How do we teach all followers of Jesus to live life as a Sabbath gift—to play with God in the Garden? What does it mean to please God with our hearts, minds, and spirits in every age of our lives? What does it mean to engage in Godplay in each age of life?

> *Let us go forth with fear and courage and rage to save the world.*
> GRACE PALEY

In the First Age, pleasing God becomes an embedded posture that bears fruit in every phase of life. In the First Age, what pleases God is our taking the time to toy and tinker with life, learning Jesus "by heart" and our part in his mission in the world, and playing in the dirt and makeshift art of that native clay. Our soul is only the clay; it must be shaped into something, or it remains "globulus" and not art. It is the church's responsibility to help people climb inside the story, make the story their own, and live the story. A story or metaphor, charged by the Spirit, buries itself and takes root in the soul, where it grows, blooms, and bears fruit throughout life's mission.

If you know your mission in life, then what other people have and do and say about you does not matter. But if you have no mission, or don't know your mission, then what other people have and do and say about you matters a great deal.

In the Second Age, what pleases God is participation—in our calling and chosenness, in our community of followers, in our walk with Christ. The Second Age is a time to "get real" about our vocation and our faith, best done through education as enchantment, and to start "rocking" the world with our story. It's a time to relearn how to play, how to get down and dirty, and how to start singing in a confident and powerful voice the song God made us to be. It's a time to play hard and dream big. We have all been "called" to live out our gifts. The quality of our participation in God's calling for our lives and our chosenness for ministry and mission are the defining Godplay of the Second Age.

In the Third Age, what pleases God is the maturing of our lives to the "full stature of Christ,"[54] wherein we take pleasure in bearing the fruit that pleases God most. It is the time of our greatest freedom—freedom from the fear of others' judgments as well as our own attempts to manipulate them.[55] Note how the landscape of winter reveals the shape of things better than any other season. Everything in winter becomes so much clearer: our trees, our shrubs, our lives. The winter of life reveals the true shape of the soul.

But maturing doesn't mean we stop playing. On the contrary, it means we have the savvy and *sprezzatura* to be game changers![56] In other words, the Third Age is the best age of our lives. Godplay is our pleasure in the walk that charts new paths, cuts new valleys, grows new trees, and isn't afraid

◇

Bless to me, O God, the earth beneath my foot,
Bless to me, O God, the path whereon I go;
Bless to me, O God, the thing of my desire;
Thou ever-more of ever-more,
Bless thou to me my rest.
Bless to me the thing whereon is set my mind,
Bless to me the thing whereon is set my love;
Bless to me the thing whereon is set my hope;
O thou King of kings,
Bless thou to me mine eye!
As thou wast before at my life's beginning,
Be thou so again
At my journey's end.
As thou wast besides at my soul's shaping,
Father, be thou too at my journey's close.
Be with me at each time, lying down and arising,
Be with me in sleep, companioned by dear ones. Amen.[57]

ANCIENT CELTIC PRAYER

to play the field. If you are not leaving life with the sense of unfinished business, then your "business" was too paltry and puny to begin with.

There is an old story of a hardened crusader accepting a bet from another soldier who insisted that it was impossible for him to carry a flame from the Church of the Holy

Sepulchre in Jerusalem back to Paris. On the reverse pilgrimage from Jerusalem to Paris, he had to guard the flame from robbers and storms and stumbles and other vicissitudes of life. But in the process of living with the flame and becoming its protector, his heart was changed from a calloused soldier's heart to a gentle, sensitive, compassionate soul. His whole desire changed—from winning the bet to protecting the flame. By the time he arrived in Paris, no one who had known him before recognized him. He was a totally changed person. As the legend goes, he arrived on Holy Saturday, and it was his flame that lit the paschal fire that year.

In the Third Age, the fire of the gospel is in the hands of master players and marquee mentors who can teach others how to play well, not as players of their own game, but as players of God's Great Game of Life. The Third Age is when we can finally "master" moving from the world's "work" paradigm to a more biblical "play" paradigm, where true artistry and creativity is born. The end of human existence, the ultimate meaning of life, the secret to happiness, is found in two words we have cast asunder that were meant to be joined together: *God+play.*

In every age of our lives, we need to tap from deep within the sense of God's gift of *play*—the consciousness that in every part of life, everywhere we look, in everything we do, we can experience God's pleasure. When our lives become Godplay, we can hear echoing in ourselves the assuring words Jesus heard at the Jordan River: "You are my beloved. You bring me great pleasure."[58]

Life is not work. Life is play.

PART I

Playing Is Not Just for Children

1

THE WORLD IS MY GARDEN

"They heard the Lord God walking in the garden in the dew of the day. And the man and the woman hid themselves from the presence of the Lord God amidst the trees of the garden.

"Then the Lord God called to the human, 'Where are you, Adam?'

"'I'm hiding.'"[1]

Adam and Eve played hide-and-seek in the Garden with a God who does not lie hidden, a God who can be seen and heard, talked to and walked with. Hide-and-seek is not the game we were created to play. If anything, God is the seeker and we are the hiders.[2] "Seeker-sensitive" worship was rightly named, but wrongly focused on the human rather than the divine.[3] We don't need to travel to find Christ. Christ has already traveled to find us. God is not the one whose back is turned. It is we who, for whatever reason, get our backs up or don't turn back to God.

Humans were designed to walk and play with God in

the Garden without shame, reveling in the joy of Godplay. In freedom's Fall, we exchanged a play paradigm for a work paradigm. But if we are to live as we were created to, bearing the image of God, we must seek to return to the art of play. Humankind was created to live a Garden life. We were made to play with God the game of "tending and tilling the soil," or as I prefer to title it in the game of life, "conserving and conceiving" our relationships with God, each other (*nigh-boor* is "the person who tills the patch of ground next to ours"), and the world. Unfortunately, too often we have turned the Garden game of "conserve and conceive" into a gambling addiction called "consume and casino."

Jesus, the second Adam, came to replace the game of hide-and-seek with a new game—"to seek and to save the lost"[4]—and to lead us back into our natural Garden habit(at) of playing with God. Jesus calls to us with the "shepherd's voice." When we hear the Good Shepherd's voice and follow it, we find our way back into the welcoming and forgiving arms of God, who beckons us into the place of joy and intimacy we long left behind. God's Garden is play-full not work-full. To please God is to embrace not the world's work fetish, but the Garden's playground. If faith isn't fun, we're working for God rather than playing with God. Instead of a Protestant work ethic,[5] we need a Paradise play ethic. In one of the greatest ironies in Christian history, the Protestant work ethic did more to support "works righteousness" than almost anything ever invented by the Roman Catholic Church.

The Spirit does not stir our hearts to produce *works* so

much as to produce *faith*, *hope*, and *love* within us. God is not interested in showing the world how we can work, but in how we can love and laurel the gift of life, how we can laud the One who is Life. The mark of the early church was not, "See how well they work!" but, "See how well they love!" The prevalence of love signals the presence of play. When faith

———— ◇ ————

The only purpose in life is the search for God.

TIMOTHY LEARY

becomes all about *beliefs* and *works* instead of *relationships*, then what we're really in love with is our own thoughts and opinions and doings—not an image of God, but an image of ourselves.

A play ethic does not suppress or deny the hardness of life, nor is it a flight into the arms of cheap grace. Rather, playing with God is the ultimate act of faith in God's promises and hope in God's providences to bring about a dynamic present and an even better future. To trust God in order to *get* something is not faith, but self-interest. Faith is trusting God because of who God is—trusting God when there is nothing to get, when everything is gone, when only God is left. Playing with God frees our faith to trust, to receive the gifts of life, and to advance joy for all people.

Another reason why we need to move to a play ethic and away from a work ethic is that the victory has already been won, on the cross. That means, as Watchman Nee pointed out long ago, we spend too much time fighting *for* victory when we should be fighting *from* or *on the basis of* victory. There is no need to fuss and fret, despair and fear. We play on a field on which Jesus has already won our freedom. Our "labor" is part of the deceptive work of Satan, who wants us to believe that the outcome has yet to be determined. We are players in a game in which every move counts, but we have no need to count every move because we can count instead on the Prime Mover, the true Master Player.

Jesus found his security in God's love and favor. We can too. But, too often, we instead seek security in the desires and tangibles of the world: wealth, status, and public praise.

It's easy to get lost when we're working our way through life. A *work ethic* urges us to "go it alone," to fight our way through, to set out toward mirages of self-made glory—superficial paths of sheen and shimmer—in order to get where we want to go. A *work ethic* causes us to be competitive and to try to lead our own posse.

By contrast, the best *play* is never a solo act. The best children's games don't need anything more than companionship and a bit of mud and sticks. Play is a grassroots endeavor. Play gets us back to who we are. (Don't you feel more yourself just thinking about it?) And play gets fun when we acknowledge that we are not playing at life alone.

The children's game Marco Polo is a wonderful metaphor for the explorative and adventurous journey we take through life when we follow Jesus' lead. We listen for the Master's voice calling, "Where are you?" and we follow that voice until it leads us home. There are various explanations of how the game Marco Polo evolved. Some say it was inspired from a real-life occurrence in the master explorer's life.

The game Marco Polo historically refers to the time
when the explorer Marco Polo (then age seventeen)
was exploring the region of China with his father
and uncle. They were traveling to China in order
to see the Khan. Marco grew very exhausted during
their travels and fell asleep on his horse one day.
His horse sensed this and dropped back from the
traveling caravan within the nation. When Marco
woke up and did not see his family, he began to
hear voices within the desert and thought that it was
his family searching for him and calling his name,
"Marco." Because of this, he began to respond to
those cries with "Polo." It turned out that Marco
Polo was actually hallucinating and they were not
calling him, even though he was later found by his
family.[6]

Others see the game merely as a later creative adaptation of
the explorer's quest:

Many people thought Polo's explorations would
yield nothing, and just be a wild goose chase.
Therefore, the game where you blindly stumble
along (sail) in an area of water (the oceans he sailed),
looking for things (people, in the game) to get you
out of trouble (being Marco) would naturally be
named after him. . . . At the end of the game, you
find someone to get you out of being Marco, and
Marco Polo found . . . people to get him out of the

debt he would have been in if he [hadn't] brought
home riches and valuable knowledge.[7]

No matter which story is true, the truth is in the story. Games
are ways we deal with the difficulties in life. Games can also
be ways that we find our way back to our beginnings.

Anthropologist Mary Douglas, in her posthumous masterpiece, *Thinking in Circles*, discovered that ancient writings
such as the Hebrew Scriptures were written not in linear
sequences, but in circuitry. You start at the beginning, and
end back at the beginning, but not the beginning where you
began. You end at a new beginning, where you have grown
and matured, discovered something new, and found something newly valued. For us as humans, God is our "never-
ending" story. And our whole lives are spent searching to
get back to that Garden home
with God after spits and spurts at
guerrilla gardening east of Eden.

In *The Wonderful Wizard of
Oz*, the 1900 story by L. Frank
Baum, Dorothy leaves home only
to discover, after multiple adventures, that everything good and
beautiful was already there in her own backyard. Her true
promised land was not the glitz and glitter of Oz, but the relationships with loved ones she had left and had always known.
The world where she belonged was lost and then found.

Our "backyard" is the Garden of God, which stretches
through all of creation. When we start our pilgrimage and

*You can discover more about a
person in an hour of play than
in a year of conversation.*

PLATO

stay on the Garden path until the end, we don't find God by going "somewhere else," but by discovering anew the beauty of the God who is already there, in/with/among us, and inviting us to play. If our lives hear the summoning Voice to "come and see," then the world is our Garden. God's voice is calling to us from beyond the wilderness: "Come and be with me." But God does not wait for us to come. God comes to each of us. The God who comes to the world is the One who says, "Come to me" but is always coming to us.

In Hebrew culture, throughout history, the Sabbath (Shabbat) is the narrative metaphor for living a still-in-one-peace life filled with God's good pleasure. The combination of the two words *Shabbat* (Sabbath) and *Shalom* (peace) sums up everything that is beautiful about God's design for the created world and for humanity within it. Shabbat Shalom is the Promised Land—a place of total surrender and rest in God, where "all our strivings cease" and where we trust God enough to play out God's purposes in us. To hallow the Sabbath day is to live a hallowed life.

Since when did the Sabbath become synonymous with the self-help culture of health and wellness, mere psychobabble for "taking care of ourselves," "taking time for ourselves," "being good to ourselves," or "nourishing ourselves"? What happened to the Jewish idea of Sabbath, in which one finds delight in God, makes space for grace and worship, both at home and in synagogue, with ritual and food and candles and prayer?

Sabbath *sets aside* time and space for the reverence of God, so that the celebrant may find joy in the beauty of that relationship and in all relationships.[8] Even sex is revered on the Sabbath for its covenantal role in pleasing God by pleasuring one's spouse and preserving the marriage covenant. Jesus healed on the Sabbath because the Sabbath was less about ceasing "work" than about spreading *Shalom*. Perhaps the best meaning of Shabbat Shalom is conveyed not by "Peace be with you," but by "May you be fully healed and whole again, joyful and alive in the arms of God."

We live in an ironic society where even play is turned into work. But the highest existence is not work; the highest level of existence is play.

CONRAD HYERS

Disciples of John fasted. Disciples of Jesus feasted. Whose disciples are we? As Timothy Radcliffe notes, "The monastic discipline of fasting was not so much about *not* eating, as being at ease in eating, eating what was put before you, eating together in gratitude, eating no more than your body needs."[9]

Shabbat literally means "ceasing from work or labor." What was meant to be forbidden on the Sabbath were those activities that we would call "work" or "skilled," those things that control and change rather than fit in with God's natural order. It is not best translated as a "day of rest," which connotes cessation of activity. Rather, it is a "day of play"—a day of fun, family, games, sex, praise. It is a festive day, a holy day, a holiday that everyone looks forward to and leans into. It is a time for remembering what God has done, and a foretaste of the messianic age to come. It is the creative space to attend to life's subtleties—what Steve Jobs called "listening to the whisperings."[10] Shabbat is celebrated with three festive meals, with sparkling conversation, with music and dance, and with luxuriating in our relationship with God. It is a day that returns us to the Garden.

In a Talmudic legend, the Sabbath does its own version of the Jewish "oy veh!" shtick, moaning and groaning before God about how all the other days of the week were given a mate, except the Sabbath. "Very well," the Lord is said to have replied, "the Jewish people will be your groom." The Sabbath and the Jewish people are then united in wedlock, bride and groom, with God as the matchmaker.[11]

In Jewish tradition, Shabbat is *Kallah*, the bride, and prayers abound with references to the meat, bread, wine, and oil used in the wedding banquet. As one prepares for the bride, so the people prepare for Shabbat. As one longs for the arrival of the bride, so the people yearn for the coming of Shabbat. As the departure of the bride brings sadness, so, too, does the close of Shabbat.

In the Jewish tradition, every instance of life, every moment of

———————— ◇ ————————

Thank God that there are solid folk
Who water flowers and roll the lawn
And sit and sew and talk and smoke
And snore through all the summer dawn.
C. S. LEWIS

existence, is an exercise in holiness. From a Jewish theological standpoint, there is no secular act. There are only activities that we have not yet perceived in all their holiness. *Play* opens up our eyes to the sacredness of the ordinary—to the majestic sanctity of the mundane, the everyday, the common.

Jesus enabled us to experience the pleasure of Shabbat Shalom in every part of life. He also let us know that God bestows this gift on all people. We are all chosen, Jews and Gentiles, all beloved, all blessed to receive God's favor and to be made whole and nourished from God's bounty. Whether we can receive this gift depends on our willingness to trust the Holy Spirit. Some see the Spirit as a divine string puller. I see the Holy Spirit as a divine wire cutter—freeing us from the shackles that bind and blind us so that we can live what Mary DeMuth calls the "uncaged life."[12]

Without the Holy Spirit's bypass surgery on all that blocks life, freedom, and joy in our lives, we cannot experience the pleasure of a life lived in perpetual Shabbat Shalom.

2

FOLLOW THE LEADER

EVERY JOURNEY IN LIFE is a Great Walk, a Garden walk with God. It is a Shabbat Shalom adventure, brimming with unexpected plays, places, and people. Jesus Pilgrims are people who don't always know how to follow or where they're going, but they know who they're following and going with. In fact, for Jesus followers, the path is not a trail, the path is the person.

The discipleship path, sometimes known as the Emmaus Road, is not meant to be hard: "My yoke is easy and My burden is light."[1] But we are warned that the road will be narrow,[2] like a narrow bridge, tightrope walk, or jungle path. We should not expect the opulence of wide, cleared swaths or eight-lane superhighways. If Jesus is our only Pathfinder, we should expect to hack new walkways through deep underbrush and encounter teetering suspension bridges. But only on this road do we encounter daily Emmaus revelations, where we suddenly realize that Jesus has been walking alongside us all the way.

The Emmaus Road is a lifelong pilgrimage that is meant

to be a shared, not solo, adventure. Not a once-and-done determination, discipleship is a daily walk of daring that takes the pilgrim on strange paths and untried paces in different ages. For some, these ages may be consecutive stages. But for all, the art of Garden walking with God keeps us in covenant relationship from birth through death.

—— ◇ ——

The whole world is nothing but a very narrow bridge. The main thing is not to be afraid.

RABBI NACHMAN OF BRESLOV

A fly is a perfect example of the status quo. Young or old, a fly doesn't change, and it remains the same size throughout its adult life. Even after death, it does not rapidly decompose. Too many followers of Jesus are living a "fly gospel" that produces nice people rather than saints; that stands for convention rather than adventure; that is respectable rather than passionate; that calls for guarded, take-care living rather than heroic, take-risks living; that is more at home with the status quo than with living on the fly.

To drive rich trades at the bank of heaven requires not more work, but more play.

The Great Walk is not a Bible study. The Great Walk is a Spirit-filled life of Godplay that includes Bible study, prayer walks, and many more such Sabbath-play activities (not "works") that ensure we are not "strangers to the covenant." If prayer is our first priority, then the rest of life falls into place. Prayer is life's ultimate play. Prayer is the DNA of the play revolution.

Barbara Jurgensen, in one of her books, tells the story of Excelsis Smith and his most obstreperous small niece.

Whenever Smith fell heir to the task of babysitting the young girl, his wits were taxed to the utmost, answering her questions and inventing ways to keep her unrelenting mind entertained.

One Sunday morning he had taken her to church, thinking the hymns and Scripture passages and sermon would keep her thought processes occupied without his help for an hour. But the respite was short. She emerged from the church full of questions.

"The sermon was on the Holy Spirit," she began. "What is this Holy Spirit?"

"Well," he said, "the Holy Spirit is a person, a part of the Trinity."

"I know all that, but what does he do?"

"Well, he lives within each Christian, helping him to live as a follower of Christ."

"Are you a Christian?"

"Yes."

No longer do we take the sword against any nations, nor do we learn war any more since we have become sons [and daughters] of peace through Jesus who is our author instead of following the traditional customs, by which we were "strangers to the covenant."

ORIGEN OF ALEXANDRIA

"Then do you have the Holy Spirit in you?"

She had caught him off guard.

"Well, I . . . what do you mean, do I have the Holy Spirit in me? Do you mean, can I feel him in me?"

"No, I just mean do you have the Holy Spirit in you?"

"Well . . . I . . ."

"If you are a Christian," she went on, "and Christians

have the Holy Spirit living in them, then you must have the Holy Spirit in you. Right?"

"Well . . ."

"That must be a wonderful thing," she said, "to actually have the Holy Spirit living in you."[3]

In the Bible, the Spirit sometimes "comes upon" someone (e.g., King Cyrus, Samson, Gideon, etc.), for a purpose, for a moment, for a mission. But what the Spirit really wants is to "live within" someone, to take up residence in someone's life until he or she lives a Spirit-filled life and even becomes a Hercules of the Holy Spirit. That's a whole different experience of the "coming of the Spirit."

◇

May God free me from my wickedness,

May God free me from my entrapment,

May God free me from every gully,

From every tortuous road, from every slough.

May God open to me every pass,

Christ open to me every narrow way,

Each soul of holy man and woman in heaven

Be preparing for me my pathway.[4]

ANCIENT CELTIC PRAYER

The Great Walk is a 1^3 (one to the third power, which means power upon power upon power) pilgrimage of Spirit-filled discipleship.

The first "one" in the 1^3 Great Walk refers to a slow walk. In technical terms, a slow walk is 1 mph. A 1 mph wind is known as "near calm" in meteorological circles. A near calm wind will bend a blade of grass, but it will also change the trajectory of a bullet by fifteen inches. That seemingly insignificant influence is the very definition of the calm, constrained, but life-changing power of prayer.

The second "one" in the 1³ walk refers to one degree of separation. Supposedly, we live in a six-degrees-of-separation world—that is, every person on the planet is separated from all other persons on the planet (all seven billion) by no more than six relationship links. The Great Walk is not a solo walk; it is done in "covenant" with others who, by virtue of their relationship with Christ, are no more than one degree of separation away.

The third "one" in the 1³ walk refers to the longest distance in the universe—the distance from zero to one. It is harder to go from zero to one than from one to any other number. The distance from zero to one is the very definition of *new*, which is at the heart of Emmanuel's promise: "Behold, I make all things new."[5] The drama of human existence, we are promised, finds its fulfillment not only in a new humanity but in "a new heaven and a new earth."[6] The question is not whether we grow old or grow young; there is another way to grow—not old or young, but *new*. The promise of the gospel is that in our walk through life, we can keep growing new—with a "new song" to sing to the drumbeat of life as we dance to a "new rhythm," make a "new heart" to throb, and allow a "new spirit" to glow, as God does in us a "new thing" for every "new day."

From the moment of birth, we head downward to inhabit

——————— ◇ ———————

Life is too deep for words, so don't try to describe it; just live it.

C. S. LEWIS

a mini-universe that begins to grow old. Everything and everyone grows old along with us, and the more we run out of days, the more we run away with ourselves and run around in ever-shrinking circles. But in the walk of faith, the recreative power of the Spirit of God rains on us daily the manna of new food that renders us "fresh every morning."[7] A life devoted to the securing of money to be hoarded and possessed ahead of the time it will be needed leads to senility and sterility. A life devoted to trust in God's provision of manna that can be gathered only each morning is life's secret fountain of youth.

If only Robert Browning had changed the second word in his poem "Rabbi Ben Ezra" from *old* to *new*, the poem would have been perfect:

> Grow [new] along with me!
> The best is yet to be,
> The last of life, for which the first was made:
> Our times are in His hand
> Who saith, "A whole I planned,
> Youth shows but half; Trust God: see all, nor be afraid!"[8]

No wonder we do not lose heart on The Way—even while fighting gravity's battle of the bulge, lumbago, bifocals, bridges, baldness, bunions, and other barnacles of aging. Though our outward humanity is in decay, we are inwardly renewed day by day by the manna—the mystery food—of the Spirit. Evelyn Waugh described the story line of his novel

Brideshead Revisited as "the operation of divine grace" on the human heart. But it's an "operation" that takes more than an hour or a day. The soul surgery of *grace* takes a lifetime to complete.

"Following the leader," when the leader is Christ, is to allow ourselves to be nourished without worry, to face life with the spirit of a child, and to go with Jesus no matter where the path leads us. It is to live a Sabbath-Shalom life, to revel in the creativity of play that allows the adrenaline rush of confronting challenges, and to have the endurance to go the distance. In Christ, our course will be one of not just a destination, not just a journey, but as anthropologist Mary Douglas suggests, of growing into new eyes and new senses. Yes, even "growing new."

As we mature in discipleship, we don't grow *old*, we grow new in Christ. We become *fresher*, more in tune with the Holy Spirit. As we give ourselves up to Christ, we *grow into* a renewal of the soul that allows us to feel the joy of "child-likeness" in the Lord.

There is another secret to growing new. We might call it the paradox of true newness: The only way to get it is not to go after it. As we give up our need to re*make* ourselves, we become re*newed* in Christ's image. Like happiness that pops up as a by-product of worthwhile pursuits, newness is found in giving ourselves away by sacrificing for others.

If we pursue novelty, simply tracking the trends, we will continually be let down . . . continually be depleted . . . continue to grow old because we are not being renewed with real food—the Living Bread. But if we live out of our wisdom, our discipleship, our relationship with Christ, out of our Christian maturity, and seek to embrace our time of life in relationship with the changeless image of Christ, our aging will become instead a constant renewal, a replenishment, a new life in Jesus that makes us as pure and new as a child in the eyes of God.

Seek novelty and we grow old. Live out of the old and we grow new.

———————————— ◇ ————————————

Blessed be the Child Who today delights Bethlehem,
Blessed be the Newborn Who today made humanity young again.
Blessed be the Fruit Who bowed Himself down for our hunger.
Blessed be the Gracious One Who suddenly enriched all of our
* poverty and filled our need.*

ST. EPHREM THE SYRIAN

3

WALK THE RED CARPET

IN THE CLOSING PAGES of Bob Hope's bestselling memoir about his then fifty years in the business, *Don't Shoot, It's Only Me*, he answers this question: "After all these years, why don't you retire and go fishing?"

"Fish don't applaud."

Bob Hope wasn't the only one hungry for applause. In some ways, we are all applause seekers, more dependent on the approval of others than we would ever like to admit; more inclined to be people pleasers than God pleasers. When we place our sense of self in the reflection we see in other people's eyes, what happens when those other people go away?

At our worst, we are not at all the prophetic and grace-bearing people of the "coat of many colors," pleasuring and basking in God's favor. But like the peacock and its similar nonrelative, the bird of paradise, we love to strut our own colors with glitz and glitter down the runway of life. Our "self" has fallen more in love with its own appearance than in loving "Christ's appearing."[1] Our church is less "hidden with Christ in God"[2] than hiding Christ while crowing and crowning itself. "Come to Christ" has devolved to "Come to church."

The male bird of paradise has gloriously colored plumage. Those with the longest, thickest tails attract the most females. Subsequent offspring also exhibit the long tail and also compete well for females. Unfortunately, the birds with the biggest tails also have the biggest problem escaping predators who appreciate large birds pinned in place by their plumage. So the bird with the most sex appeal is also the worst choice as a fit mate. Not unlike high school . . . or the rest of life.

---------- ◇ ----------

One final word, friends. We ask you—urge is more like it—that you keep on doing what we told you to do to please God, not in a dogged religious plod, but in a living, spirited dance.[3]

PAUL THE APOSTLE

Life is not a catwalk. It's not a runway for us to strut our stuff and receive the admiration of the crowds. Honor is not found in honors; happiness is not found in having; well-being is not found in wealth. Neither is life a sightseeing excursion, in which disciples approach their time on earth as touristic travelers. For a follower of Jesus, life is a pilgrimage. Even more precisely, life is a processional, a "walkathon" designed to be a festival of praise and dance celebrated by all those walking in the way of Christ.

Dom Jeremy Driscoll is an American Benedictine monk who talks about the monastic tradition of processions.

"Monks are always having processions. As a community, whenever we go from one place to another, we don't just do it helter-skelter; we go in procession. We process into church; we process out. We process to a meal. We process to our cells. We process to the cemetery. We process around our property."[4] In other words, a pilgrim's walk is going somewhere. Pilgrimage is not ill-defined movement through life, but a key chapter of a larger story, a vital song in the unfinished symphony of salvation, a march of mission that is part of the epic procession of Christ through history and through time, leading to that final movement for which we watch, wait, and make our way as pilgrims.

The way we process through life determines not just how soon we arrive at the end point of our procession, but how we find highs and high points in the walk itself. The joy of the Lord depends largely on who we're pilgrimaging with.[5]

An Olympic athlete who had been seriously injured needed to heal gradually and then learn to walk again. He became very discouraged and depressed until he met a coach who set about to help him with his healing. One day the coach told the athlete that he would show him something very cool if only he would climb a nearby mountain with him. So they climbed the mountain. The athlete made it to the top and looked around. Although the view was astounding, he wanted to know what was so special.

"This is it," the coach said.

The athlete became angry and said, "I thought there would be more to the destination than just a beautiful view." The coach replied that it was never about the destination, but about the joy of the pilgrimage. We may be "destined" for the heavenly Kingdom, but it's what we do and learn in this life, how we play out our discipleship journey, that bears the image of Christ in this world.

If life were only about the journey, we'd all be born as amblin', ramblin' men and women.[6] But life is not merely about the destination either. Life is, most important, about the joy and dance of the procession, the sport of the "walk-athon," and who is walking that pilgrimage with us. We have spent five hundred years in the "Here I Stand" mode of Protestantism. Maybe it's time to move to a "There We Go" mode of mission. In other words, "Take a Hike." The Christian life is a journey narrative . . . a road trip. And Godplay is a group hike.

I grew up in the Pilgrim Holiness (now Wesleyan Church) and Free Methodist traditions, which preserved the covenant renewal services John Wesley started in 1740. Popularly known as watch night services, they were a Protestant rein-vention of the vigils that historically preceded holy days with liturgies of holy readings, psalm singing, silence, and brief homilies (often excerpts from the church fathers). In Methodist hands, the watch night service was a sober alter-native to the revelry of Christmas Eve and especially New Year's Eve. Concluding just after midnight, the Sweet family celebrated the arrival of a New Year by renewing the cov-enants we had made with God, with each other, and with ourselves and by public storytelling (called "testimonies") of what choices had detoured us, and what right roads we had taken during the concluding year.

The watch night tradition is worthy of rediscovering. But to be drawn to the dawn, where death and destruction are defeated, is a unique kind of vigil. It's a processional of covenantal vigilance in contributing to a victory that has already been won. It's a "watch" and "wait" by participants and players who don't just watch and wait. Pilgrims are called to be as concerned with the here and now as with the world to come. In fact, part of watch night is to invite eternity into our homes and communities now, and to maintain high standards of hospitality for the future in the present. When Jesus offered eternal life,[7] it did not just mean life for eternity or immortality, but the life of the Eternal One starting here and now.

In the past, Christian homes kept ready what was called a "prophet's chamber" for entertaining traveling preachers. Perhaps today we need to keep a prophet's chamber for entertaining eternity, for hosting the Kingdom of God, for watch night readiness that continually renews the vows of our covenant.

We think to be strong is not to be beholden to anybody. We think to "stand on our own two feet" is to stand alone. In this "culture of control,"[8] we want to take care of ourselves and direct our own destiny. This posture may gain attention for a while, but it won't keep us warm in the night, it won't help us dance with others, nor will it take us in any worthwhile direction or to any meaningful destination.

Living in the pleasure of God requires a dependence on God and one another that is frightening to mortals too proud to be needy. The richness of human existence is grown not in the topsoil of our precociousness and "strength," but in the humus of our neediness and vulnerability. It isn't "free spirits" or "broken spirits" that have breached the covenant the most from the beginning of time—but "independent spirits." Pride doesn't just "goeth before a fall." Pride *is* the Fall. People with their noses in the air are more likely to trip and fall. Pride is what first ended our daily walks with God in the Garden. God is pleased with people who let God be God, not proud people[9] who like Adam and Eve, clamor after the divine portfolio. Truth be told, we have "out-Adamed" Adam in our deep-rooted, drum-rolling, all-controlling pride.

Perhaps the most famous project to come out of the Enlightenment was Denis Diderot's *Encyclopédie*, published in France between 1751 and 1772. In Diderot's explanation of his project, he contended that the *Encyclopédie*'s raison d'être was to bring all the knowledge of the universe together in one place, "to change the way people think," and "to put person at the center of the universe."

The Enlightenment Project, another name for "the modern world," got it half right. "Person" does belong at the center of the universe, but the modern world chose the wrong one. *You* don't belong at the center of the universe. *I* don't belong at the center of the universe. The human self is not the center of the universe. Only Jesus belongs at the center of the universe.

Being in relationship with God, admitting our dependence on God, means being in recovery from our control addictions. Recovery is so difficult that we would do anything else to avoid it—make strict rules and rulers to hold us to strictures and toe the line of regulations, create impersonal ministries and missions, devise rituals and illusions to *appease* instead of *please* God.

God pleasing is neither a marathon of deeds nor a competition for celestial goodies and cookies. God's pleasure is a mantle bestowed as a gift. This is what it means to be *blessed*: to be invited into a relationship where you are not the controller, but the receiver. The robe of righteousness, more play clothes than Sunday dress, is not worn or carried as a burden, but as a blessing. The yoke of Christ is designed to make our work easier, shared, more playful, and creative. It is the banding between Christ and his bride. Our walk with Christ is a lovers' bond, as we carry the cross together across every obstacle and through every opportunity.

———————— ◇ ————————

There is always a tendency to call the lower groups of society the worst sinners. The street-walkers, the beggars, the outcasts, the robbers and the drunkards are the usual scapegoats. The real sinners, however, are those who pride themselves on being otherwise.

JOHN RAWLS

As John Wesley lay dying, in his eighty-seventh year, he gathered his friends around him, spoke his farewells, and lifted his feeble arms in this blessing: "The best of all is, God is with us."[10] When the worst hits our lives, Godplayers are those who celebrate life's best: "The best of all is, God is with us."

We all have a date with death. We just have no idea when our date will arrive. The question is, how will we be dressed when our date arrives? Will we have "put on Christ"? Will we be dressed in Christ's robes of righteousness? What will we wear when we take up residence, as each one of us must, in the Terminal Café? Will we be able to say, with the writer of Proverbs, "Strength and dignity are her clothing, and she laughs at the time to come"?[11] In guarding our holy places with laughing, mocking creatures called gargoyles, griffins, and grotesqueries, our ancestors realized that the best way to deal with devils, diseases, and death was to laugh at them.

We do not *measure* our walk with God as much as *pleasure* in it, like the lovers' stroll through a garden in the evening breeze. We dig up the Kingdom as we play in the dirt with God. We don't *earn* a place in Christ's Kingdom based on how many miles we cover in a day, how many fields we can plow in a season, how many seeds we plant, or how much muck we can dig up with our backhoes. We are *gifted* with a walk that we can either take or turn down. In life, the way we walk, and whom we choose to walk with, shows our true identity. When we walk with God, we let God's light shine. Or we ought to. There's enough religious slime and ecclesiastical moonshine out there. It's time for some Jesus shine—the pure love light of God radiating in the lives of God's people.

◇

Live the kind of life that pleases God, who calls you to share in his own Kingdom and glory.

PAUL THE APOSTLE

Sometimes, Godplayers shrine the shine, focusing the light on the light itself. Other times, we need to let it burn.

The metaphor of the *covenant* features two key components: (1) fruit bearing, propagation, and birthright—passing the baton of faith to the next generation; and (2) the relational tattoo (a covenant is always *cut*) that signifies special identity as *favored* and *follower*. The walk of God is both the lovers' stroll that lingers and the marriage processional that goes ever forward to multiply and mature. It contains the kernels of both self-emptying and self-sacrifice, Bethlehem's cradle and Calvary's Cross. For those of the old covenant, to "walk with God" meant to be in right relationship with God so that one lived a life that showcased God's grace and other attributes of the covenant. For those of the new covenant, walking with God means to walk with Christ (as little "Christs") and spread the joy of that walk to the ends of the earth.

The Spirit came upon the disciples when they were "of one accord." What does it mean to be "of one heart and one mind"? It means to have the heart of God, the mind of Christ, and a harmony of spirit—but not a homogenous spirit. To be in covenant means to walk "in accord," or to be bound in harmonious deference to the score of the Creator, and to be "in tune" with Creation's music of harmonious differences.

Consider the similar but different lyrics of the song of David, the song of Deborah, the song of Esther, the song of Moses, the song of Solomon, and most pointedly, the greatest song ever sung, the Song of Jesus.[12] The walk "with God" or "before God" is one that does not hide sin or self, does not seek other paths or paragons, and does not deviate from the truth, but stands exposed and humbled before Jesus Christ, divinity distilled into a singular birth and a truth-is-stranger-than-fiction story. In fact, to confess you're a sinner and in need of a Savior is to tell the truth about your story and to not feel the need to hide behind Photoshopped or politically correct versions of yourself. In a sense, the covenant with Adam is one of humble dependency from the start. (*Adama* means "from the dirt" or "from the ground up.") To recognize our neediness—to live in the daily breath of God's Spirit and the daily bread of God's promises—is to live in *adama*.

One day, in a moment of silly exuberance after viewing a Honda commercial, I played with the word *accord*, which most people know only as the name of the bestselling car in the United States.

To be in Holy *ACCORD* is to be in . . .

Adoration, Connection, Communion,

Obedience, Relationship, Deference

Holy *ACCORD* is to walk not in defiance but in *deference* to our Creator. To *adore* God with our love and respect; to strive to stay *connected* at all times; to seek *communion* with Christ to the depth of our souls; to love *obediently* with all our heart, mind, soul, and strength; and to stay in *relationship* with Christ in every phase of life. When we pay attention to God's presence and respond to that presence with holy "accord," we walk with God. As we walk with God, we experience God's good pleasure.

⬦

I will walk among you, and will be your God.

LEVITICUS 26:12, KJB

Godplay is a call to rise. To rise up and walk as we stand up and make a stand. To get on your feet with dignity and grace.

At the Beautiful Gate of the Temple, a beggar asked Peter and John for some money. Peter spoke these words to the beggar: "Look at us . . . I have no silver or gold, but what I have I give you: in the name of Jesus Christ of Nazareth, stand up and walk."[13] The purpose of every gift, whether silver or gold, prayers or blessings, is the same: helping someone to rise to their feet, stand up straight, and walk.

But before any healing takes place, there is a bidding: "Look at us."

Too often, we look at the problems of the world with our eyes closed. Before human need can be outfaced, we first must look it in the face. We must stare it down and confront it boldly.

"Look at us!"

At the moment our eyes truly meet human need, the miracle happens.

Just as Jesus was raised from the dead, we are to raise others from death to life. But after helping people rise up, we must stay with them for a while, as Peter and John did, to help them get steady on their feet. Godplayers are the "risen" people whose mission in life is to gift others with the joy of a "risen" Lord as we journey through life.

4

CAVE DWELLERS

If I were to ask you to tell me a cave story, I bet you'd have one. Not as memorable, perhaps, as the one told by Prisoner 46664, who spent eighteen of his twenty-seven years in prison hewing stones in and out of the caves of Robben Island off the coast of Cape Town, South Africa. There, Nelson Mandela's ideals of mercy and reconciliation were honed with every strike of the hammer that broke the rocks—rocks broken for no other purpose than to break the spirit of the prisoners. Constant movement from pitch blackness to glaring sun caused Mandela's eyes to be burned to the point where he lost the ability to cry, even after he was released. But his suffering in the caves of Robben Island taught the world to cry.

Think about it. We all have our cave stories. They may be from a visit to one of the cave parks that can be found in virtually every region of North America, or from our first step into the mouth of a cave we discovered while hiking near home. Caves make huge deposits in our memory banks and in our souls.

Here is a cave story from the original Renaissance Man—
and arguably the most talented person to have ever lived—
Leonardo da Vinci:

> Drawn by my eager wish, desirous of seeing the great
> confusion of the various strange forms created by
> ingenious nature, I wandered for some time among
> the shadowed cliffs, and came to the entrance of
> a great cavern. I remained before it for a while,
> stupefied, and ignorant of the existence of such a
> thing, with my back bent and my left hand resting
> on my knee, and shading my eyes with my right,
> with lids lowered and closed, and often bending this
> way and that to see whether I could discern anything
> within; but this was denied me by the great darkness
> inside. And after I stayed a while, suddenly there
> arose in me two things, fear and desire—fear because
> of the menacing dark cave, and desire to see whether
> there were any miraculous thing within.[1]

The wilderness of Judah is filled with caves, and the Bible is
full of cave stories: the caves of Adullam, Engedi, Makkedah,
and Machpelah, to name but a few.[2] The cave of Machpelah
is the burial place of Judaism's three patriarchs—Abraham,
Isaac, and Jacob—and three of its four matriarchs—Sarah,
Rebekah, and Leah. The word of the Lord came to Elijah in
a cave,[3] to Paul in a cave,[4] and the Word-made-flesh was born
in a cave and buried in a cave.

The Judean hills and the mounds of Samaria are riddled

with natural caves, most used to shelter animals, but in cold weather humans sought shelter there as well. The more primitive the cave, the more likely to find animals only—and usually an eclectic mix of cows, sheep, donkeys, and goats. Cave floors were often carpeted with dried dung, and millions of fleas found a home there, ready for any unsuspecting flesh to leap onto. These caves were more sordid than any slum. Even cavemen didn't live there.

We have images of cavemen as savages who lived in the Stone Age and did nothing but search for food by day and sit around fires grunting and trying to stay warm by night while being stalked by saber-toothed tigers. The truth is that the cavemen didn't live in the caves—they lived in artificial shelters; but they used caves and rock overhangs for ceremonial purposes and artwork. Even cavemen were artists.

◇

The true object of all human life is play.

G. K. CHESTERTON

Leonardo da Vinci was right: The descent into the darkness of a cave (the Greeks called it *katabasis*) is a journey of both *womb* and *tomb*, pregnant with the promise of creativity and enlightenment, but also gestating with unknown terrors of cave-ins and ground-giving-way entrapments.

G. K. Chesterton, one of the greatest Christian apologists who ever lived, turned his cave story into a parable:

A man who was entirely careless of spiritual affairs died and went to hell. And he was much missed on earth by his old friends. His business agent went down to the gates of hell to see if there was any chance of bringing him back. But though he pleaded for the gates to be opened, the iron bars never yielded. His priest also went and argued: "He was not really a bad fellow, given time he would have matured. Let him out, please!" The gates remained stubbornly shut against all their voices. Finally, his mother came; she did not beg for his release. Quietly, and with a strange catch in her voice, she said to Satan: "*Let me in.*" Immediately the great doors swung open upon their hinges. For love goes down through the gates of hell and there redeems the dead.[5]

Chesterton's cave story is a parable of the Incarnation . . . and of every incarnational ministry since Jesus. Every pilgrim is a student of cave life, a spiritual speleologist who seeks out the cave dwellers for rescue and redemption and who carries with him or her the "ark" ("cave box") of the covenant. In fact, Jesus himself, the Ark of the New Covenant, became a Cave Dweller to release those trapped in underground living and to robe those willing to follow him into the darkened caves and condominiums of this world with the pure cloaks of righteousness. In his life, death, and resurrection, Jesus played a deeper game than even his disciples realized.

Who will enter the caves of redemption? They are as filled with treasure as Aladdin's caves—though not with armoires of gold and silver or underground labyrinths of stalactites and stalagmites, helictites, "soda straws," gypsum threads, cave pearls, cave popcorn, aragonite bushes, gypsum flowers, or "chande-liers." Caves of redemption are treasure chests of lepers, the demon possessed, the dropsied, bent women, babies, beggars, little ones, mothers-in-law, tax collectors, soldiers, prostitutes, the insane, and other misfits and outcasts waiting for Love to open their prisons.[6] Jesus the Cave Dweller, who welcomed "sinners"[7] into his cave, makes every mountain sacred and turns caves of death into caves of new life and coves of prayer, feeding these underground caves and coves with the purest springs of water from deep within the mountain.

◇

Play is kissed by infinity because, whether it involves creating a work of art, playing a piece of music, relaxing among friends, or entering into the mystery of the liturgy, it transports us into an altered state of consciousness within which our sense of time and space is dissolved, our rational mind loses its grip on our senses and feelings, and we become aware of the presence of God as an irresistible mystery beckoning to us within and beyond the horizons of the known and knowable world.

TINA BEATTIE

But we must be willing to play with God in deep and dark places, listen to the "still small voice"[8] that echoes at the mouth of caves, the place where mysteries are not solved but resolved into deeper mysteries, a place where we must release our grip on belief and surrender ourselves to faith, a place where we must "give up everything that does not lead to God,"[9] confining but defining places where we can be fashioned into God's image and share in God's own nature.

There is an old fable about some people who heard of a place called "cave of truth." They discussed this among themselves and finally decided to set out in search of this cave. After a long and difficult journey, they found it.

At the entrance sat an old man who was the guardian of the cave. The people asked him if they might enter. In reply, the guardian asked, "How deeply into the cave of truth do you want to go?"

At this question, they retreated and talked among themselves. When they returned, they said, "We would like to enter and go just deep enough to be able to say, 'We have been there.'"

The cave of the covenant inexorably draws us into something deeper. The covenant is designed for extreme spelunking, for deep play. For Godplay.

Wise spelunkers have learned a certain precaution. Before entering an unknown cavern, before they venture to play among the stalactites and stalagmites, they tie one end of a spool of cord to a tree or rock outside the cave. As they make their way through the labyrinthine passageways, they unwind the cord, knowing that it will always lead them back to where they started. In the cave of the covenant, our one safety is being *tied* to the Tree of Life, the Rock of Ages—*tied* to Christ.[10]

The Garden walk with God takes us outside to play, with the whole world as our playground. Playing with God is an incarnational pilgrimage with relational requirements as well as missional directives.[11] Life's pilgrimage is a prayer walk in which we pilgrims live the three Ages of life in an ever-changing landscape of the Spirit: deserts, mountains, seashores, valleys, caves, rivers, jungles, forests, night skies.[12]

Whatever landscape your soul finds itself in, that landscape changes when the storms come. These thunderstorms, tornadoes, hurricanes, monsoons, ice storms, whatever, will come out of the blue; others are self-produced. Either way, they're your storms, and only you can get through them. The question is whether you will ride them out with Jesus or try to ride them out alone. It's one thing to play with God in the light. It's another thing to play with God in the dark—or, like Mother Teresa, to build arks in the dark.[13]

Every organic thing is planted for the future. But for a plant to reach the future, it must grow in two opposite directions at the same time. As the roots grow downward into the dark, into the depths, the plant's limbs reach for the light and grow upward. Birth and rootedness take place in cave-dark spaces, from which grow the upward, outward expression. No darkness, no light. No dirt, no daybreak. No past, no future.

Humans are a unique species because we can bring together into one conscious collage three explicit existences: *past*, *present*, and *future*. Animals live their lives in the present, by habit and instinct; humans dream and design theirs in ways that bring the three existences together.

Followers of Jesus always find themselves playing on two fronts. The pilgrim journey of playing with God is one that is both rooted and shooted, both backward and forward, both spiritual and corporeal, both unseen and seen. The dance of tradition and innovation, continuity and change, memory and imagination, is the pilgrim way to move through time.

True nobility of spirit is not just confessing our sins, but also retracing our steps and acknowledging our debts to our sources and sponsors. Our ancestors are ballasts of identity and wisdom. Who says you can't "go back"? Of course we can go back. We go back by incorporating into the present the traditions and collective wisdom of our ancestors. Tradition keeps us from going overboard and keeps everything aboveboard. The interplay of newfangled and old-fogeyed creates a style of living that is both trendy and traditional. Like old marching bands that step back before stepping forward, we live in the present from the past forward.

The mission to "be fruitful and multiply" is given first to Adam and Eve, then to Noah and his sons, and then to all covenant-keeping descendants of Abraham.[14] The invitation to multiplication is not intended only to reproduce the human creature, but also to propagate (to seed and reseed) the story of Yahweh within humankind and propagate the covenant relationship throughout the generations. The story and image of God is what is multiplied—and thereby magnified.

In the New Covenant, Christ's identity as Truth is also clearly evident in the invitation to discipleship:

> Abide in Me and I in you. As the branch cannot bear fruit of itself unless it abides in the vine, so neither can you unless you abide in Me. . . . Apart from Me you can do nothing. . . . My Father is glorified by this, that you bear much fruit.[15]

Christ's directive to his disciples, then, is one of mission and multiplication:

> I am the way, and the truth, and the life. . . .
> Therefore go and make disciples.[16]

All of these statements are covenant statements—the first, within Yahweh's covenant with the Hebrews; the second, within the New Covenant of Jesus Christ with humanity. Both are the same covenant. The Son of God serves within the second covenant as the gateway connection to God.

Brennan Manning is one of my favorite authors, and one of my favorite stories about Brennan is tucked away in the About the Author section of his book *Abba's Child*:

————— ◇ —————

Whether you turn to the right or to the left, your ears will hear a voice behind you, saying, "This is the way; walk in it."

ISAIAH 30:21, NIV

> A two-year leave of absence from the Franciscans took Brennan to Spain in the late sixties. He joined the Little Brothers of Jesus of Charles de Foucauld, an Order committed to an uncloistered, contemplative life among the poor. . . . Among his many and varied assignments, Brennan became . . . a solitary contemplative secluded in a remote cave for six months in the Zaragoza desert.
>
> During his retreat in the isolated cave, Brennan

was once again powerfully convicted by the revelation of God's love in the crucified Christ. On a midwinter's night, he received this word from the Lord: "For love of you I left my Father's side. I came to you who ran from me, who fled me, who did not want to hear my name. For love of you I was covered with spit, punched and beaten, and fixed to the wood of the cross." Brennan would later reflect, "Those words are burned into my life. That night, I learned what a wise old Franciscan told me the day I joined the Order—'Once you come to know the love of Jesus Christ, nothing else in the world will seem as beautiful or desirable.'"[17]

If you're a Jesus follower, you're an acolyte and laurel-bearer of the world's greatest lover.[18]

PARTYING IN GOD'S ADVENTURE STORY

THERE IS AN OLD SAYING that there are two kinds of people in the world: those who go to a party and don't want to leave, and those who go to a party and can't wait to go. Unfortunately, these two kinds of people are usually married to each other.

I'm of a third kind of person: I don't go to parties in the first place. I hate parties . . . but I love to party. I feel a kinship with the poet T. S. Eliot, who once replied when asked whether he was enjoying himself at a party, "Yes, if you see the essential horror of it all."[1]

The "horror of it all" lies in the fact that, for most people in attendance, they aren't true parties. They're more like the peaks of meringue on a lemon pie—an attempt to create pinnacles of sweetness from a sour, soupy, flat existence. This is what propelled Lillian Hellman, who suffered the last five years of her life from a debilitating heart disease that left her frail and panting, to go to parties, even when she had to go in an ambulance.

But for those in love with Jesus, those engaged in Godplay, life is more like swimming in a sea of living water. Fresh and clean, you can drink as you ride the waves. And when you are surfing the waves of the Spirit, all of life is a party. In the same way that Jesus can make all of life a mission trip—not just one outing—he can make a vocation and vacation one and the same. He can make all of life a grand adventure.

A party is a place where we do nothing but greet old friends, meet new people, and enjoy one another. Jesus set up a party theme early in his ministry, with his coming-out miracle at the wedding in Cana and with a slew of party-crashing and missed-party stories.[2]

The Gospels serve up a feast of feast stories. Is it even possible to read them without getting hungry? Jesus always seems to have food in his hands—from his first wedding feast to his last supper . . . and then those Resurrection meals. The Gospels are one giant block party. In many of these party scenes, Jesus eats as readily with publicans and prostitutes as with the cocky Pharisees and the colossally rich. You might even say he came to cross party lines with party times. If we deleted all the parties from the Gospel of Luke, where "the Son of Man came eating and drinking,"[3] it would be a mighty thin book. One of the (many) criticisms of Jesus was that he enjoyed life a little too much.[4] Have you been criticized for excessive celebration recently? Is it possible that God moves as much at a party or barbecue as at an ecclesiastical service?

I suspect that a prime reason why Bethany was Jesus' favorite place on earth was because he enjoyed Martha's cooking. The problem was that feeding Jesus had become *work* for Martha, not play. She had gone from the joy of cooking to the burden of cooking. The Bread of Life yearns to be fun: not workspace for the stressed, but Play-Doh for the spirit.

Most of us are like Martha: too busy to party. But we are proud carriers of BMB Syndrome (Behold Me Busy), also known as the White Rabbit Hurry Sickness: "I'm late, I'm late, for a very important date. No time to say hello/good-bye—I'm late! I'm late! I'm late!" Life is not meant to be a full court press.

Our hardscrabble ancestors who toiled from dawn 'til dusk, and sometimes from dusk 'til dawn again, were afraid to embrace pleasure and play due to its distracting potential. But there was an insidious theological rationale for their solemnity, expressed in a popular spirituality text from a hundred years ago:

◇

If there's room in the heart, there's always room in the house.
MABEL BOGGS SWEET

> The spirit that opens the gates of heaven longs for the coming of Jesus, . . . and would gladly never have any physical pleasure but for the legitimate needs and recreations of the body. In the language of the wise man, "It eats for strength, and not for the mere pleasure of appetite."[5]

For a long time, and for too many today, the natural attire of a Jesus follower is sackcloth and ashes (the latter to be sprinkled on ice cream when it tastes too good).

Before much of the church sold out to a muted and moderate Gutenberg culture of words and propositions, Christianity itself was a celebratory culture of feast days and carnivals and festivities where artists of various media were employed to design architectural settings, paintings, music, clothes, food, sporting events, dancing, speeches, liturgy, movement. Festivals were as dynamic and dramatic, authentic and lunatic, noisome and fulsome as life itself. When people think of plays, they think of somber, serious stage presentations. But "plays" were festivals. After Shakespeare's plays, even performances of *Julius Caesar* and *Richard III*, people in the sixteenth and seventeenth centuries left Shakespeare's Globe Theatre clapping, tapping their feet, and dancing along with the players.[6] If life is played with adventure and a partying spirit, life itself becomes a festival culture, a fandango of faith, where we leave our seats skipping and dancing to the tune of the Creator.

One of the greatest party passages in the Bible is Paul's challenge to "love one another with brotherly affection; outdo one another in showing honor."[7] That last phrase, "showing honor," means to celebrate people with meat, drink, sweets, and wreathe them with laurels. A party is a place where we meet and play and celebrate: meet for the sheer joy of being together, play and revel in relationships, and celebrate those who "play" important roles in our lives. When life is *played*, not worked, the fantastic is just around the corner, and the "fantasy" life is already in this one. It is found in the relationships we form, foster, and fete with one another. As the light of the stars is lost in the dawn of the morning, the need to be the life of the party fades when life is a party.

Celebrating the joy of everyday living is only the beginning of our adventure with the Lord of all life. Discipleship is a lifelong journey. But more than that, it's a grand adventure story—the kind of story with surprises around every corner and games down every path. It combines the joy of relationships with the perils and excitement of new discoveries. It challenges our stamina and rewards our endurance. It celebrates our spirit of play and blesses our creativity. Life is a festival of joy with Christ at the front of the procession, his voice resounding above the rest: "Come and see!"

In whatever age you're in . . . to wherever places your pilgrimage takes you, from First-Age tinkering to Third-Age world changing, just keep following that voice: "Come and see!"

I once had a student whose daughter, in one year, went from being deep into SpongeBob SquarePants to being deep into Jesus. She wanted a Jesus birthday party . . . with Jesus cake, Jesus candles, Jesus napkins, Jesus balloons, and, "Mom, can we have a Jesus piñata?"[8]

No one is more tired than I am of seeing Jesus turned into a piñata for hacked-off people to hack away at to their hearts' delight. But certain clichés about Jesus *are* piñata worthy—and I give fair warning: I have just now become a hacker.

> *Creation is a bird without a flight plan, that will never fly in a straight line.*
>
> VIOLETA PARRA

One of the biggest clichés in the church today has provided legions of people with untold comfort and consolation: "God has a wonderful plan for your life."

I like a good cliché as much as anyone, but when truth

becomes captive to a cliché, it's time to hack our way through the underbrush of presumption. Are you ready for the whack hack? Here it comes . . .

There is no *plan*. God didn't give us a plan, but a purpose; not a map, but a mission; not a blueprint for tracing, but a blue sky for exploring. God's *plan* is for us to spend our lives doing whatever unlocks our tear ducts, makes our throats deep with song, keeps the gales of laughter surging in our souls, and turns our feet to dancing.

What next?

If you can answer that question for your life, whether based on your reading of the Bible or tea leaves or goat entrails (like the Greeks at Delphi), go ahead and plan. The verb form of the word *plan* means "decide on and arrange in advance."

If you can't answer the question, *What next?*, then eat your humble pie (the "umbles" were the entrails left to people of lesser importance) and enjoy your vocation as a partner in providence. Nothing happens as planned. Or in the words of an ancient sage, "The mind of man plans his way, but the LORD directs his steps."[9] So, prepare, prophesy, hold on to your seat, and play to your strengths as you delight in the sandbox life of *Ludens Dei* ("God at play").

God did not create us to live out a "life plan" or a "master plan." There is no one plan with definite specifics. God has made us with special gifts and blessings, with the expectation that we enjoy using them in God's mission in the world, the "reign of God." Or as Augustine put it in such memorable form, "Love God, and do what you will."

When we kiss someone, we don't left brain it; we right

brain a kiss. We don't analyze a kiss before we do it, or plan it out according to some rule of thumb. We just make it up as we go along, following the signs, signals, and feedback loops of the one we're kissing. We "kiss" life the same way.

At certain times in our lives, the journey will be more *Canterbury Tales* than *Pilgrim's Progress*, but if we don't know where God is calling us to go, we might end up someplace else. And where God is calling us to go is always and everywhere toward the Christ who is always anywhere and everywhere. The course of our lives is charted by the coordinates of Christ, and as any navigator will tell you about the headings of a course, the coordinates must be checked consistently—at least hourly. We don't need a map when Jesus is our GPS (God Positioning System).

Just as there is no requirement that a river follow a certain course to be true to its source—a true course, whatever its path, is simply one that flows to the sea—so, too, has God set us free to flow, to play, to take pleasure in our relationship with God, and to glorify and enjoy God. That freedom allows us to take risks and enjoy the journey.

US Army Special Forces training is now based on how to improvise and find your footing in unstable circumstances, not on how to devise and adhere to a plan.

Everyone who understands economics is in retreat from the dangers and constraints of a "command economy." In China, the preferred expression is "planned economy" (*jihua jingji*), but it means the same thing. And the Chinese are becoming more entrepreneurial and quick on their feet than those "Western capitalists."

A "planned" life works no better than a "planned" economy. In a world where the half-life of information is steadily decreasing, the road to hell is paved with strategic plans and best practices.

God's *plan* is to always be there to pick us up. No matter how many bad things happen to us, God can turn those bad things to good. Grace turns the very things that brought us down into the means of lifting us higher to help others see broader vistas of God.

Try this. If it doesn't play, try that. God will always be there for you. We all fall. But when we fall, we have a fall-back. God will be there—in, with, and under the stuff of our lives—every step of the way, for as long as it takes and as many potholes as we hit. That's the *plan*—that we will arrive eventually and never be alone as we journey along the way. That's the plan: "The losses and crosses are better means to growth in grace than when everything is according to our liking" is how John Wesley put it.

God's plan, simply stated, is this: *"I've got you covered. I'll be there for you."*

No matter how bad things are or how big a mess we make, God's plan is to never leave us or forsake us. In other words, God's "plan" is really a *promise*.

But we can't leave it there. We love the promises but forget the particulars. Yes, Jesus promised, "Ask whatever you will, and it shall be done for you," but those words are framed by an important context. Here's the full quote: "If you abide in me, and my words abide in you, ask whatever you will, and it shall be done for you. By this my Father is glorified, that you bear much fruit, and so prove to be my disciples."[10] So, "It shall be done for you" (1) in God's good time—hence "abidance"; (2) for God's good pleasure; and (3) for the purpose of our bearing good fruit.

The Bible is not the story of how to plan or what to expect in life, but the story of what not to expect in life—dead men walking, water turning to wine, missions impossible, etc. The Bible is not the story of "great expectations," but "great unexpectations." This is why I get so frustrated when critics say, "But dead men don't walk, but you can't turn water into wine, but that makes no sense . . ." They're missing the whole point. The Bible is not the story of how to live life "normal," by the numbers, by the book. It's the story of how to live life *by the Spirit*. The Bible is the story of what it is to live an anything-can-happen life.

In short, God's love is not a plan but a story, a story of love that is stronger than death. What makes the story unpredictable is that God invites us to author parts of it ourselves.

That's not to say that God is some distant, deistic being who has abandoned the love story. I trust that God is up to something *big* in this theodrama, and that we fit into that larger story in some way that will always escape us. I trust also that God will intervene and act and love us personally; that anything small enough to worry about is big enough to pray and talk to God about.

"God is in control." Well, yes, that's called Providence. But Providence doesn't mean we can't mess things up terribly, and ruin our lives, and destroy other people and the planet. "God is in control" only means we know how the story ends.

"Everything that happens is for the best." Not true. Everything that happens is decidedly *not* for the best. But the providence and sovereignty of God can bring to the best everything that happens.

What's better than a divine *plan*? Divine providence, divine protection, and divine promises.

PART II

First Age (0–30)
Novice Player: Toying and Tinkering

6

A STORY WAITING
TO HAPPEN

WE LEARN TO CRAWL before we learn to walk. But we learn to *play* the moment we enter the world. We wiggle our toes, we laugh, we coo, we make faces. We love music and colors, exploring and discovering, and story after story. We were created to have a sense of play imprinted on our souls—much like the Inuit hero Smilla has a "sense of snow" imprinted on her childhood, in Danish novelist Peter Høeg's international bestseller.[1] But somewhere along the path, our native sense of *play* and *story* gives way to an overlay of *words* and *work*.

The 1940 Walt Disney film *Pinocchio* begins with the opening of a storybook. From that parting of the pages, one crosses over into a magical land of fantasy—along with the invitation to become part of the story. Sally Lloyd-Jones opens her *Jesus Storybook Bible* in a similar fashion. It's one of the best book openings I've ever read:

> The Bible isn't a book of rules, or a book of heroes. The Bible is most of all a Story. It's an adventure story about a young Hero who comes from a far country to win back his lost treasure. It's a love story about a brave Prince who leaves his palace, his throne—everything—to rescue the one he loves. It's like the most wonderful of fairy tales that has come true in real life!
>
> You see, the best thing about this Story is—it's true.
>
> There are lots of stories in the Bible, but all the stories are telling one Big Story. The Story of how God loves his children and comes to rescue them.
>
> It takes the whole Bible to tell this Story. And at the center of the Story, there is a baby. Every Story in the Bible whispers his name. He is like the missing piece in a puzzle—the piece that makes all the other pieces fit together, and suddenly you can see a beautiful picture.[2]

Jesus is history's Master Storyteller. He taught with story, he played with story, he healed with story, he loved with story. He showed us the truth of God's love in the stories of the Hebrew people and in the story of his own life. Jesus, the Last Adam—or better yet, "Adam . . . at last!"—"orients" us eastward, in the direction of the Garden, the primal Ur story of God's love for us.

Charles Wesley prayed that God would "arm him" to "serve the present age." He had in mind, of course, Paul's "arming" in Ephesians. He wanted the "sword of the Spirit," which is the preparation of the gospel of peace. If we want to be armed in the resistance movement against the barbarians at today's gate, what are our armaments? Doctrines, propositions, or stories? The real "sword drills" for kids are not who can cite or recite the verses first, but who knows the stories best.

For First Age Godplayers, stories are the bread and butter of life. "Bring up children in the way of the Story, and when they are older, they will return to it."[3] First Age is a time of learning the stories from the texts and traditions of our faith, narratives and metaphors (narraphors) that provide a base identity from which to "go outside and play."

———— ◇ ————

Play is the creation of value that is not necessary.

DALLAS WILLARD

Identity needs narrative form and expression in order to be strong and real. Identities based on words and principles are weak. Identities based on narraphors and practices are strong. Established rituals of practice in storytelling and storyhearing bring a certain litany and rhythm to life. Out of that "groove" come a security and confidence of identity that can overcome our limitations and set us free from our fears.

The major developmental agenda of the First Age is *identity formation*. The question of identity is "Who am I?" God's question to Hagar in the wilderness is the primordial question of identity: "Where have you come from, and where are you going?"[4] God's question of Hagar conflicts with the prevailing wisdom to "start from where you are," which often means "ignore the past," or even worse, "tear up the roots." One of the hazards of hypermodernism (which some people call post-modernity) is not just a faddish tendency toward universal amnesia (besides a lack of passion, lack of humor, lack of . . . I could go on and on). But what memory there is tends to be an ironic, even disrespectful, knowingness of the past.

The identity question of "Who am I?" needs answering in the context of human formation, which is a lifetime assignment. The tragedy is that our culture is becoming better than the church at bringing the two together. Every company and institution that has literally, and not just figuratively, entered the twenty-first century is reinventing itself around "who we are" as opposed to "what we sell." For followers of Jesus, "who we are" is never answered in terms of what we buy, but by what we contribute; it's never our collections, but always our connections. Christianity, it seems, still needs its best idea to be explained to it.

As parents, giving our children the freedom to choose their faith is like telling them to choose their language. At birth, parents naturally choose their children's verbal language. At baptism, parents choose their children's faith language. When children are born into a family, they learn the family name, identity, traditions, practices, life line, and character. Shared stories and songs create collective identities. An English-speaking family teaches

---

⬦

First off, nothing . . . but God. No light, no time, no substance, no matter. Second off, God says the word and WHAP! Stuff everywhere! . . . And floating above it all, God's Holy Spirit ready to play.

ROB LACEY, *THE WORD ON THE STREET*

---

its children to speak English. German- or Spanish-speaking families teach their children to speak German or Spanish.

There is a "life story" to be told—and lived in community with others who share the same story and conjugate the same grammar. Families are designed to incubate, inculcate, and enculturate stories, even to put them into writing or capture them in photos, images, icons, mementos, and artifacts.

Families should never allow mere "things" or "stuff" past the threshold of the home. Only stories find a permanent place at home. In the Sweet household, everything either has a story or has no right to be there. This includes dishes, silverware, pictures, furniture, rugs, everything.

Only stories are the true stuff of life. When we immerse ourselves in The True Story That Is Jesus, and surround ourselves with his stories, his life-giving Story becomes our story as well, living in us over and over, in fuller measure, again and again, until our story hardly seems the same story it used to be.

I am a Wesleyan by practice, but I am a Calvinist about some things. I believe in parental predestination. From the moment I began swimming inside my mother, I was predestined for the living waters of baptism and the deeper waters of the Spirit. From my crib, I was predestined for the altar. From my high chair and potty chair, where I was taught to read and not idle, I was predestined for a library chair and an academic chair. From my bedside as a child, where my mother prayed that God would use me someday in a special way, I was predestined for the roadside of the world and the far side of the church. From kneeling each day at family prayer, I was predestined to spend my life knee-deep in the Scriptures and getting my kneecaps kicked for always taking deeper looks, always searching for deeper levels. It is the responsibility of parents to predestine (not predetermine) their children for the gospel. In parental predestination, we prophesy our children into the Kingdom while preserving their right to decide one day whom to serve. In parental predetermination, we do all we can to leave our children no choice, thereby overdetermining our children's existence.

When the "self" is God's original design for us, Shakespeare's phrase, "To thine own self be true," is another way of saying, "To God be true." But a "true self" presupposes a self-identity, which implies a self with the freedom to create itself, and a self shaped in submission to communal identities. I am who I am because I am engaged in the life-long task of becoming the person God made me, but also because I find myself in the ancestral and familial stories of people traveling on similar trajectories and engaged in similar life projects. The history of the Jews is a great example.

The percentage of the world's population that is Jewish is relatively infinitesimal. Out of a current seven billion people walking the planet, only about 13.5 million are Jews (0.2 percent). It's hard to get much smaller than that and still be measured.

Forget that number for a moment and look at the percentage of Nobel Prize winners in literature, science, and medicine who are Jews. Almost a quarter of all Nobel Prize winners are Jewish. The results are strikingly similar for Pulitzers, Oscars, Grammys, Fields Medals, Kennedy Center honors, patents, and copyrights. The measure of Jewish achievement in any arena of life that commands creativity, innovation, imagination, or entrepreneurship is stunning. The disproportionate impact on the arts of the Jewish demographic is especially staggering.[5] How different are the sound tracks of our souls with the playlists from two Jewish troubadours, one Canadian and one Minnesotan: Leonard Cohen and Robert Zimmerman, aka Bob Dylan.

The question always asked, and sometimes studied, is this: Why has humanity's advance through history been so dependent on contributions of Jewish creativity and imagination? What is their secret to releasing into the bloodstream of history such creativeness and resourcefulness?

We now know. In fact, it's very simple, but very profound. In what setting do the most sacred moments in the Jewish faith take place? In temples? In synagogues? No, in the home. Where in the home? At a table. And who presides at that table—a rabbi or priest? No, the elder of the family. And what does the elder do at that most sacred moment? Tells the stories. The central episode in Jewish history is celebrated not in a synagogue by priests, but in the home by parents, around a table set for an evening meal, serving up a story as the main course.

This isn't just so that those seated at the table can learn the stories or take the moral pill inside the narrative pudding. It is a religious requirement of Judaism that these stories become each and every generation's stories, that every child be able to see himself or herself in the sandals of Moses standing up to Pharaoh, to the point where the child "becomes" Moses.

Jewish children are given the privilege of viewing themselves as if they had come out of Egypt, to so identify with Hannah and Samuel, Abraham and Sarah, that they become Hannah and Samuel, Abraham and Sarah. Then and only then have they really *learned* the story.

The theological fulcrum in Judaism that makes light all this heavy lifting is the Hebrew word for "remember" (*zakhar*). *Zakhar* conveys two things missing in much of our "remembering" today. First, in Hebrew, remembering is an essential task that involves the discharging of debts. In other words, remembering is a responsibility, not a choice. Second, to remember means more than bringing something from the past to mind. It means bringing the past to present reality. It means to live in the present out of the remembered reality of the past. It means to "re-member" ourselves to the story, even if we've been disconnected from the story or have dismembered ourselves from the community. When we remember the Exodus story, we make that story come to life in the present and live out the reality of freedom. When God "remembers" the covenant, it means the covenant remains operative, no matter what humans do. Neither God nor we can declare bankruptcy. The covenant entails the discharge of a debt to the past, with the sense that we are born debtors and die even more in debt.

It is in this sense, then, that every Jewish child, from day one, is given an identity. From the stories of the faith, every Jewish child is told who he or she is.

Now compare that rich narrative foundation with the circumstances of most Christian children, who, after being raised on weak narrative diets in the home and church, are encouraged to take their bare narrative bones into the posh cultures of consumerism and celebrity and "find yourself" or "discover who you are."[6] When we leave our kids to forge an identity for themselves in the culture, who is waiting to help them create this self-identity? Out of what do they fashion their identity? Out of "mass-mediated images" generated by consumer culture. There are at least three things wrong with this: First, they're *mass*, not homegrown, or artisanal; second, they're *mediated*, not hands-on or handed down; third, they're *images*, not real life or the real thing.

Jewish children don't need to invest precious intellectual and psychological resources in the essential developmental task of identity formation, which in a consumer culture becomes a sinkhole at best, and a cesspool at worst. Sufficiently secure of their seat in the saddle, Jewish First Agers can invest their creativity and imagination in more constructive and playful pursuits, and this has resulted in some of the greatest creative forces in world history.

Even when they, for whatever reason, are removed from their Jewish faith, or are remote from religious observance, their narrative identity holds. "Next Year in Jerusalem" can be spoken as a religious hope or as an imaginal endeavor. "Let my people go!" is a hinge of Jewish history, or it can be a hinge of human history. In a world that always tries to "take out the other," the Jews—the ultimate *others*, the always *others*—survive on the enduring power of their story.

There is one more feature of this narrative identity that helps to explain the Jewish contribution to world history.

Jewish children are not just expected to *learn* the story and *live* the story. They are also expected to *question* the quest. In fact, it's an act of reverence to ask questions of the story. The Jews are confident that the story is strong enough to be tried and tested, prodded and pricked, taken apart and turned inside out. Questions are as sacred as answers, and the act of questioning the story may be as close as Jews come to a sacrament.[7] It is from within this background that Jesus became the Master Questioner of history, asking almost twice as many questions as he was asked.[8]

In Christian circles, always raising questions ensures that one is rarely invited back. In Jewish circles, raising questions is what gets you invited back. The juiciest fruit of the academic endeavor, that of asking more questions than you can answer, is bitten into at every Jewish table. In fact, it is almost a Jewish commandment that no question worth its salt is answerable. A worthy question generates new questions along with old and new nuances of answers. Around the table, a Jewish child has "That's a good question!" drummed into his or her soul, not, "You don't ask that question."

This culture of "sporting debate" is reflected in Judaic paintings of Torah scholars arguing rambunctiously with one another and gesticulating wildly around a Torah scroll. Some things are not an answer; they're a start. And sometimes we need starts more than we need answers: baby steps in the right direction.

Another community that has managed to maintain its identity and retain its children is the Amish. Ninety-five percent of Amish youth remain Amish, even after a trial period of permissive "roaming around" called *rumspringa*. A few years ago, I spent some time in the heart of Amish Country—Sugarcreek, Ohio, the highest concentration of Old Order Amish in the United States. I received a special gift of being allowed to attend "the Singing," a courtship ritual that takes place every Sunday night. This is the Amish equivalent of a "youth group."

The Singing begins with a buffet supper, and this is the only time the kids eat first while the parents and elders watch and eat last. While taking the food, boys on one side of the table, girls on the other, the youths exchange greetings and get to know each other. The big question of the evening is always which boy gets to drive which girl home in the buggy. The one buggy I'll never forget was hot-rodded up with multiple lights—all run by battery, of course.

The Singing is built on the *Ausbund*, a hymnbook dating to 1564, which along with the Bible and a storybook are the three books that all Amish have in their homes. Perhaps the oldest Protestant hymnal in continuous use, the *Ausbund* is really a supplemental volume to *Martyr's Mirror*, a thousand-page storybook (the Anabaptist version of Foxe's *Book of Martyrs*) detailing how the Amish ancestors died for their faith. The *Ausbund* is filled with sixteenth-century martyr ballads and other prison songs written by those awaiting execution.

From infancy, Amish children are taught the stories and the songs from all three books, along with the Dordrecht Confession of Faith (1632), which outlines the basic beliefs the Amish strive to uphold today. Every Sunday at worship, hundreds of Amish congregations sing the same second hymn (#131 in the *Ausbund*) at the same time, connecting their voices in space and time through "Das Loblied," written by Leonard Clock in 1590: "O God Father, we praise you and your goodness exalt."

Four verses of this single hymn can take twenty minutes to sing—that's twenty minutes to sing 120 words. The Amish are opposed to the world's "fast tunes," although they do allow the young people to sing a little faster at the Singing.[9] There are no musical notes in the hymnbook; the music is part of the memory of the community, a memory that resides for the Amish in the whole body of the community, not just in an individual's mind.

The stories and metaphors of Christian faith are not options to be chosen, but a heritage to be bestowed. The stories of Jesus are our past, our present, and our future. The most important gifts that parents can give to their children are an identity as God's child and the security of knowing they belong to a Story much bigger than themselves.

My preacher mom, Mabel Boggs Sweet, believed that her three boys belonged "in" the world but were not "of" the world. So we were enrolled in the public school and learned the "ins" of the world, without participating in some of the "outs," such as dancing (a physician's "excuse" exempted us "for religious reasons") and games that involved cards or dice. But at the same time, she homeschooled us in Christianity, where we learned what it meant to be "of" a faith tradition (Wesleyan holiness). Granted, that tradition was transmitted to us in verse and word form, not in story and image. And that tradition kept kicking us out of its churches (blame my mother's wedding band, my father's television set). But still, we inherited an identity as part of a faith tradition that connected us to God's Story and showed us how our story and God's Story connected and belonged together. From the time we are swaddled until the time we lay down our tunics and enter into God's holy house and Garden, naked and unimpaired, our lives either conform to or resist these stories and metaphors.

We live in a data-deluged world. If we put all of the data swirling around in our world onto DVDs, the stack would stretch to the moon and back again. But what kind of stories are these? How do we teach First Agers not to just float aimlessly in a chaotic sea of data and signifiers, but to sail in the safety of a secure vessel powered on the breezes of the Holy Spirit? First Agers must be taught how to deconstruct the narratives of the culture and to recognize the hidden "narratives" behind all the images they encounter in the world. You might call this kind of education "imagacy training." As our parents taught us "literacy," we must add to their learning "imagacy." Literacy is needed for the reading of books. Imagacy is needed for the interpretation of the thousands of image communications that besiege us daily. The images you "open," the stories you choose, will determine your identity.

"Don't click!" may be as important a commandment for Google-bound First Agers as "Don't steal" has always been, if identity formation and character formation are to go hand in hand. The Internet is often filled with more sugar and cream than coffee, and children need to be taught which is which, and which is good for when and where. Though a little sugar can help the medicine go down, as Mary Poppins used to say, or give us a boost of energy, we will end up with dentures, diabetes, and a very fleshy death if we build our diet on unrestrained sugar.

The images that feed us messages by the mouthful each and every day are not all bad. But they can tease, tempt, taunt, and tirade us into "clicking." Once we do, it's over. Our reputation, our computer, our hard drive is ruined. If you think *words* have the power to soil and spoil the soul, think again. *Images* are much more powerful to capture the soul and addict the body with their seductions.

Have you ever made soup and accidentally put in sugar instead of salt? Or made a cake and put in salt instead of sugar? It matters what images you choose. If you succumb to the addictive power of images, you can, in a single click, lose your identity and character amid the onslaught of viruses and identity thieves that seek to lay you to waste. Everything saved could be lost. Only a long journey can bring you back to where you started before the click.

Evil must not be reduced to weakness or displeasure or bad moods. Some days everything within me says, "Bless the Lord, O my soul, and all that is within me, bless his holy name." Other days I can't scare up a "Hallelujah!" to save my life. Other days there isn't an "Amen!" within a thousand miles. Other days my only beatitude is a bad attitude. Other days I thrash through deep water only to end up beached on muddy, miry clay.

Evil is radical alienation from God and other people, and the distance between good and evil can be tissue thin and issue broad. There is nothing good that cannot be distorted into evil.[10] In trying to escape evil, we can bring evil into the world.[11] "Think about these things," Paul writes as he itemizes a list of things that are true, just, beautiful, and pure[12] on which we can click. No one is free from thoughts of evil, but we can be exempt from evil thoughts. The former come from without; the latter from within.

We must learn the stories of Jesus to tell them. Storytellers must be story snatchers and story makers first. First Agers need Second Age and especially Third Age mentors to play and pass on the stories of Jesus so that they can build up the ID-protection they need for their own expeditions to cross fjords, hike mountains, wade streams, and swim oceans.

Our stories are like bug-catching lights. No one can avoid bugs, or live in a bugless environment. On the contrary, Jesus pleased his Father by doing exactly the opposite: He went into the most unconventional places and spent unconscionable amounts of time with the most

Prayerfulness and playfulness reverse the deadening effects of sin-determined lives.

EUGENE PETERSON

undesirable, "buggy" people with "buggy" beliefs. His light was the beacon that drew them, the laser that healed them, the flame that zapped the forces of evil, and the lightning rod that illumined the celestial coordinates in the dark.

But in order to teach "little ones" to walk, we must do what Jesus did with us—come down to their level, crawl along with them on our backs, and wrap ourselves together in the blanket of God's Story, a Story that never gets old.

In the Hebrew tradition, young children are given their first *tallit* (a tunic, or what we call a prayer shawl) as a sign that they are covered by the Torah. To be wrapped in Torah attire is to signal your identity as someone so surrounded and protected by the Scriptures that they become part of who you are. Jewish children "wear the stories" from swaddle to grave. The Christian equivalent is baptism. The Master Potter must have wet clay to mold beautiful clayware. What keeps your clay moist? Baptism, and remembrance of baptism, is the definitive moisturizer. Unfortunately, much of the original meaning of baptism has been lost.

In Christian theology, we are "divinized" twice: by birth and by baptism. In the early days of the church, baptism went by two names: *katharismos* (the cleansing of the soul) and *photismos* (the enlightening of the soul). The baptized were the "washed" and the "enlightened"—water people and fire people. Baptism and enlightenment were one and the same event. At baptism, we become clean and we become enlightened, which explains why to this day in some parts of Christianity it is the custom to give a baptized baby a white cloth and a candle as christening gifts.

By the second century, writers such as Justin Martyr, Irenaeus, and Clement of Alexandria were as likely to refer to the sacrament of baptism as someone being "enlightened." Justin Martyr writes that as Jesus was going into the water for baptism, "a fire was kindled in the Jordan"; Tatian's *Diatessaron* describes Jesus' baptism as a "great light" in the water. At baptism, your body becomes a temple of the Spirit, a vessel through which God flows and in which Christ lives and lights up. The community of the baptized, whether that community is anabaptized, water baptized, or dry-cleaned, is an open channel for the free flow of God's living water and illuminating fire in the world.

The stories of Jesus teach First Agers to love the light, to incarnate the light, and to walk in the light. Without time spent in the "playstation of light," we go through life never knowing how bright and beautiful that light can be. By teaching First Agers the stories and metaphors of the faith, we teach them to play and walk with God in the Garden. To enjoy dressing up life in the metaphorical apparel of the Scriptures. To become pilgrim players in the world, carriers of the Story. We bind them with ties, both sentimental and (more important) sacramental, to the fleeces of our ancestors.

When children walk, they walk behind or alongside a parent—or someone older, larger, wiser. Sometimes children run ahead, but as parents we try to keep them within arm's length, always where we can see them. First Agers must be taught to stay within the wide "arms" of God, to run no further than an arm's length distance away in their discipleship. The more we stay within an arm's length of our narrative identity, the easier it will be to find our way home.

7

HALO

I HAVE SPOKEN TWICE NOW at Great Britain's Youth for Christ convention, where a thousand First Agers (eighteen to thirty) from all over the British Isles gather for three days—once in a Welsh castle, once at the Royal Court Hotel in Coventry. I came away with one hallmark impression of my time there: It's one big party. For 24/7, these kids enjoyed one another, learned from one another, conversed about better ways to reach other young people for the gospel, worshiped God, and discussed theology even when they were eating (and while I was trying to talk about sports). Now that's a party!

Protestants especially are good at cerebration but poor at celebration. Generally, followers of Jesus have forgotten how to play. We drive the play out of our children with dismissive comments like "that's just child's play." We warn them that "in adulthood, everything requires work. Marriage, parenthood, parents, staying in shape, listening to music, having a garden, holidays, dinner parties, 'fun' of all kinds (except the vices . . .), to say nothing of work itself: They all require work."[1] But when we're too big to sit at the children's table, we're too big to sit at God's table.

Fledgling disciples need wings to fly *and* roots to fasten if they are to live missionally, relationally, and incarnationally in the world. Our natural habitat is the world, not the church. Jesus sent his disciples out into the world with only clothing and staff. Yet that was all they needed (with their airborne yoke and anchoring roots).

The church is the face of Christ, but only Jesus is the face of God. In the past, the face of the church has been the Avenger, determined to root out all transgressors and transgressions, as Archbishop Thomas Cranmer made clear in 1552: "Fornication and unbridled lusts of every kind are to be checked with great severity of punishment, so that they may eventually be uprooted from the kingdom."

What do people see in your face? When people look at you, when people look at a preacher or a bishop or a worship leader or a lay leader, do they see Christ living, giving, forgiving, even when bruised, derided, cursed, defiled? Or do they see a celebrity or the manager of a bureaucratic system or a "pillar of the church" on patrol, punishing wickedness with "great severity"?

My parents took seriously the Puritan understanding of the family as the "school of souls." One of the mantras of my childhood was a promise from my mother: "Boys, I don't want to isolate you from the world, but I'm doing my best to insulate you." That insulation—that "homeschooling of the soul" through family prayer, Bible memorization, twice-Sunday worship, Wednesday night prayer meetings, Sunday school, sword drills—wrapped a kind of halo around my brothers and me as we were released into the world. It was an insulation not wrapped from the outside, but emanating from within souls imbued and infected with stories of Christ.

That halo of insulation is needed now more than ever before. Seth Godin says the average person is bombarded by at least three thousand advertising messages every day. I call those messages *sermons*. When someone says they don't like preaching, I remind them that they probably listen to a couple thousand sermons every day.

◇

Christianity is a life-giving and life-transforming story before and after it is a doctrinal system.

PAUL RICOEUR

Almost every one of those "sermons" in some way preaches an anti-gospel selfology: Buy this, be happy; you're number one; you're a god; please yourself; you deserve this; you're entitled. Each one of these sermons woos its hearers to adopt its "youniversal" narrative, to follow its images, and to get branded by its logo. Each one of these sermons invites us to play God, not play *with* God.

Only a stabilizing set of spiritual training wheels on a Jesus Identity can equip First Agers and all Agers to navigate the world of competing stories. This requires a dual ability to appreciate commercial messages for their artistic genius and communication skills, yet never bite into one without a critical crunch. A resistance mentality against the prevailing status quo matures into Second and Third Age discipleship. Part of First Age insulation is learning how to deconstruct the world's messages and pull the rug from underneath their

assumptions. Followers of Jesus refuse to go gently into consumerism's good night.

Another way to think about the internalization of stories is
as a means of building in good "R-values." An R-value is the
measure of thermal resistance (resistance to heat flow) of insulation in a house or other building. The higher the R-value,
the greater the insulating effectiveness. The best insulation has
the highest R-value per inch of thickness.

We insulate our spiritual houses when we build high
R-values into our children with our stories of Jesus. As
storycrafters, in order to set up a framework of biblical
narraphors for insulating our children, we must build well-
storied structures with good protective systems of thick
insulation. Multistoried insulation regulates the "heat" of
the culture and provides a protective medium for the chaos
of images whirling about our First Agers.

Good R-values provide a level of resistance to cultural
dangers. How much resistance do you build into early followers in order for them to be in the world and not of it?
Enough to provide roots without clipping wings. Embedded
R-values are identity chips, image shapers, foundation
builders, and soul scrubbers. Like a genetic identity chip,
or homing device, they provide cleansing power, strength,
endurance, and a compass for negotiating ethical crossroads
when traveling through life's many twisted pathways.

It's like having a built-in GPS (God Positioning System)
calibrated to the heavens. With a heavenly GPS, we can
explore any territory, even the darkest places, and always
find our way home. We all lose our way at times, but good

R-values protect us and a good GPS reorients us Eastward, and Easters us home.

Good R-values are internalized identity stories . . . the Jesus Identity story. They provide the children of God identity insulation and regulation for maneuvering in the world, sufficiently secure of their seat in the saddle. Here's one example: We teach our children an ethic of words. We instruct our children in the power of "bad words" to soil the soul, and we keep those words out of earshot. My Appalachian gramma even had cleansing rituals (Ivory soap) to deal with those "bad words" when they passed from our lips. But we now live in an image culture. Images are many times more powerful to harm or heal than words. Yet we have no ethic of images, and no cleansing rituals to wash off the toxins and poisons of harmful images.

No religion speaks in abstract concepts; religion always speaks in myths, the language of image.

GERARD VAN DER LEEUW

We are witnessing an alarming decline in mental and physical health among our children, and we wonder why. We don't know for sure whether commercial media are dangerous to kids, or whether advertising aimed at youth contributes to poor nutrition and obesity, not to mention cigarette and alcohol use. But we do know that children under six can't distinguish ads from other media. At the very least, our kids need to be "insulated" by being taught media literacy (imagacy). At the very least, our kids need to be "insulated" with the cleansing practices of *hesychasm*—the exercises of silence and imageless prayer—as well as with positive images of Jesus that are stronger than any the culture can offer. Both of these may be the Google culture's equivalent of Ivory soap. If your identity is found in Christ, then it matters less and less what people think of you. Instead of allowing our kids to worry about what others think of them, we should teach them to worry whether what other people think of them is true. Truth is one place where our identity cannot be stolen.

I'd like to take you with me now into a story I call "The Tale of Iden T. Snatcher and the Storycatchers." This story is not just for kids, but especially for adults, too, because it tells—in a very "story" kind of way (or a metaphorical or parabolic kind of way . . . the Jesus way of telling a story)—how to protect ourselves with good values and a Jesus Identity when we go out not only into the real world, but also into the cyber world of social media and the metaverse.

We begin our story on a boat . . . and I invite you now to sail along with me into a sea of data and images. Our culture is in the midst of a data deluge so huge that data is reaching tidal proportions, so large that if you put all of that data on a DVD, in a single year it would reach not just around the world, but to the moon and back. The question for you Second and Third Agers out there is how to keep your kids and First Age followers (and yourselves) from drowning in an ocean of information, a tossing sea of images. How do you rear children and young adults in our twenty-first-century world not just to cling to a piece of bark in that sea or float precariously on top of it, but to build a vessel that can sail on the wings of the Spirit, across even the most choppy waves?

Just like in any tale, you have evildoers and terrible forces of darkness that will seek to drag you down into the muck and mire of the sandy depths, and when you drop your anchor from shore to shore, each "magical" site has multiple paths, secret passageways, and a plethora of buttons and turns that can lead you into all sorts of trouble.

Eventually, armed with the best insulation you can find—the super-duper Jesus Identity, you can explore the rugged terrain and spelunk through the dark caverns with confidence that *you* are a Jesus kind of Hero in a Deluge kind of World.

So, come with me now, and let's begin our journey. . . .

As you enter our boat, the *Disciple Ship*, you will notice it is insulated with some pretty powerful and important stuff—this "insulation" not only keeps the water out and seals in the warmth, but it keeps the waves from overturning the ship, and it keeps the wind from knocking down the sails. Some of the insulation is made of foam, some of rubber, some of steel, depending on what kind of places our boat needs to go. Now imagine that *you* are that boat. And the seas you are set to sail are the seas of the Internet, with its multitudinous places to visit— seas of information, waves of images, and amazing sites to see. Some may look like jungles, others like mountains, still others like rivers and oceans . . . and you need to insulate yourself well, so that you are well protected on your journey. *How?* you ask. Well, that is precisely the point of our tale . . . to show you how to maneuver this strange and new cyber world, even how to shine your light into some pretty dense and occasionally dark places . . . and come to be an expert navigator—a Jesus Super Navigator.

Our virtual world, in a sense, is like a fairy-tale world, a story set within the real story of our lives. And when we enter that storybook world, the Land of Virtuality, we become storytellers and learn to be storycatchers. A storycatcher is one who learns to capture good stories—Jesus stories—and embed them, just like data chips, into our Insulation Suit. These Jesus stories give us a super-duper new identity—a Jesus Identity—an identity that will protect us from all harm. So, the first stop on our journey must be the awesome cool Insulation Station.

Let's drop anchor and climb ashore to a little shining place (the one with the big cross on it). This is the Insulation Station, and this is where all of the stories of Jesus are kept safe from harm. When you enter, you'll see a giant virtual library, and each book is a story about Jesus. Go on now, and gather them up. And as you do, you'll find you can stick them to yourself, or even swallow them up, and before you know it, you'll start to glow from the inside out and the outside in. This is your new Insulation Suit. Never enter the Forest of Images and the Webbed Woods without your protective suit. If you do, you may find yourself lost without a compass in Which Way Maze, sinking in the Muck and Mire Swamp, attacked by Masked Marauders, infested by Viruses and Bugs—or worst of all, targeted by the Master of Evil, Iden T. Snatcher.

Iden T. Snatcher lurks within the Forest of Images, the Netted Swamps, and the Webbed Woods, just waiting for humans like you to venture into the jungle without protection. And then— before you know it—he has snatched away your entire identity. After that, even if you find your way through the Magical Forest to the Mountain of the True Master and peer into the Mirror of Truth, you won't recognize yourself. Your image will be snatched away, and whenever you look into the mirror, you will find only the images of others—and sometimes even the image of the Snatcher himself!

But when you wear your super-duper protective Insulation Suit, lined with Jesus ID chips, nothing can take your ID away, because a Jesus ID is altogether *impenetrable*!

How can you detect Iden T. Snatcher before he strikes? Well, he has a few evil helpers that you need to watch out for. For example, the Image Ghosts and the Masked Marauders. The Image Ghosts try to lure you into the Muck and Mire Swamp by flashing, taunting, and teasing you into places you don't want to go. To guard against the Image Ghosts, you'll find that your Insulation Suit is armed with a special Super Nifty X-Ray Detector. This Deception Receptor works also as an Infector Interceptor, and anytime an Image Ghost comes near, your X-Ray Detector will shine its light on that Ghost, and it will disappear in an instant. Then there are the Masked Marauders. They are a little tougher. They wear very realistic-looking masks, and they disguise themselves to look just like nice images and beautiful sites to see. But when you get there, you find they are really just fakes and foolishness. And what looked at first like a Garden of Glory might just turn out to be a Pit of Peril. For these, you need to use your special R-value Indicator. This special compass-like indicator will set you on the right road every time—it can see right through Marauder Masks and steer you far away from the Muck and Mire Swamp and the Valley of Shadows, even from Sugar Daddy Mountain. And then, Iden T. Snatcher's power will be depleted. And he will be defeated.

So, come with me now, down the Way and into the mazes. But watch what buttons you press, and what secret passageways and sites you click, and keep your super-duper Insulation Suit—your Jesus ID— on really tight. Here we go . . .

8

PLAY IN THE DIRT

WHY DO WE HAVE such an aversion to dirt? In a *work* paradigm, the task of First Agers is to dust themselves off (to get rid of the "grime" of life). In a *play* paradigm, the task of First Agers is to get down in the dirt (and revel in the nitty-gritty of life), which I call "dusting themselves down."

Dirt is our native habitat. The first time we meet God in the Bible, our Creator is making mud pies, the greatest of which is us. "You are God's tilled land," is how Paul puts it.[1] We are God's garden, God's playing field, God's mud pie masterpieces. A sandbox is the university of play.[2]

The world of the garden is filled with bugs and dirt. From the time we can walk, we love to play in the mud and muck. We go out and play, and then come back home and wash the play off. But without hands made dirty in the clay, we can't learn, create, or interact with God's world. We can lead life-friendly, unafraid lives, not because life is all clean sheets on a bed of roses, but because Jesus embedded daystars in deathbeds. The greatest dawn is often mistaken for dusk. . . . God can turn tombs into wombs, burials into resurrections.

Dirt is our friend. It is meant to play in. All gardeners have dirt under their fingernails. Without getting dirty, we can't turn soil into flower, trash bins into fruit baskets. Hands that heal touch the unclean with all their dirt and disease. Holiness is the art of turning mud and dirt into vessels of beauty, goodness, and truth. The sign of a clean heart? Dirty hands. When we come to the gates of heaven, the first thing God might say is, "Show me your hands," and the first question God might ask is, "Did you have fun playing in my garden?"

———— ◇ ————

[It's] the little things that run the world.

EDWARD O. WILSON

There is no escaping dirt. Or bugs. Or bacteria. Each one of us contains a hundred trillion bacteria in our gut—three pounds of intestinal tract lining that, if spread out, is tennis-court sized.[3] But without these bacteria, we could not digest our food.

Bugs are as important to what goes into our bodies as bacteria are to what comes out. In the United States, we spend twenty-five billion dollars a year in killing bugs, an average of two hundred dollars per person per year on repellent sprays and insecticides. But these very bugs we try so hard to kill are pollinating our plants to the tune of one hundred billion dollars per year (if we had to pay for it). Pollination is the essential reproductive strategy of the world's 240,000-plus flowering plants. At least three-quarters of these plants rely on some creature to conduct the necessary transfer of pollen. The best known pollinator is the honeybee (*Apis mellifera*), which effectively pollinates more than one hundred commercially grown crops in North America. It is the supreme pollinator, living in colonies of thousands of workers, pollinating acres of plants, and providing honey for human consumption. But the honeybee is not alone—it's not even native to this continent. For millennia prior to the bee's introduction, pollination was performed by a multitude of native insects, including solitary bees, wasps, flies, beetles, moths, butterflies, and thrips, as well as birds and a few mammals.

First Age Godplayers aren't afraid to play in the dirt, to shine their lights into caverns, to slog through swamps and valleys while wearing their halos in the world. To insulate (not isolate) is to trust our Jesus Identity for indemnity in the world. But no matter how much we insulate, we can't get rid of the risk factor. Will we put our First Agers at risk for the gospel? Will we risk their doing the right thing? To trust the story is to trust their Jesus Identity to lead them into the world, forward and back again.

Jesus said, "I am the light of the world."[4] To see the light of Christ, and to see *with* the light of Christ, is to see and shine in the dark.[5] A Jesus light can ward off evil. It can heal. It can enlighten. But only if it is willing to come outside and face the bug infested and the demonic, whether they be hiding in light or in dark places. The strongest demons reside in daylight. The buggiest beliefs can be the most politically correct.

RING AROUND THE ROSES, WE ALL FALL DOWN

FAILURE IS NOT IN THE FALLING. Failure is in not getting up again. In Proverbs we read: "A righteous man falls seven times, and rises again."[1] This is the definition of righteous humans: those who get up when they fall, not those who never fall.

We live out the story of Jesus in the world—a world not to be afraid of, a world to savor and play in. But we sometimes make falling so shameful, and the world seem so terrible, that when we tell our children to "go outside and play," they shirk from venturing far, and especially shy away from somersaults and shadows. If the world is God's Garden, then to please God is to play Shadow Living during every hill and dale of the Great Walk—to dwell "in the secret place of the Most High," to walk "under the shadow of the Almighty," and, when necessary, to hide "in the shadow of His hand."[2]

A sturdy Jesus Identity does not make us immune to falls and failures. That's why we need to provide a means of restoration for when that identity is punctured, for when people take wrong turns and get lost in the woods. We have provided First Agers too many "proscriptives"—don't, don't, don't—and too few "postscriptives" to restore and re-story them without barring them from entering the woods. We must provide ways for First Agers not only to stay rooted in the faith but also to become re-rooted in—and not rerouted from—our communities of faith.

If we cut people loose when they stumble in their footing or lose their way, we risk losing them forever. If we don't show them the way back home and welcome them with open arms to celebrate their return (remember the story of the Prodigal Son), if we do not welcome them home (remember the story of Hansel and Gretel), they will wander far into grievous places and give their hearts to fatuous but infectious images. If we abandon in the forest our runaway kids with runaround ids and IDs, the moment they pick the wrong mushroom, they will roam identity-less in a dangerous world, circling the Garden without finding their way back to God.

First Agers not only need room to roam, but permission to fail. And when they do, we need to pick them up again, straighten them up, give them a hug, and push them back out, trusting Jesus to lead them and take their hands. Our children were not meant to dwell only within the light; they were meant to shine and burn in dark places.

Of course, we can't send them into the deep darkness without a rope.

The Puritans created a massive proscriptive culture to prevent their children from stumbling. They made it as hard as possible for kids to sin. Bundling boards are a great example of this—humorous to us, but precious to them. At the same time, their theology taught them "in Adam's fall we sinned all," and that sometimes young couples would figure out how to untie the father's secret knot that kept his daughter in the sack, or find a way to lift up the bundling board that separated the two sexes in the bed. In fact, Puritan premarital pregnancy rates rival today's. Hence the Puritans created rituals of repentance and reconciliation that restored their children to the community as quickly as possible.

In other words, the Puritans made it hard to fall but easy to get back up and rejoin the fold. We live in a culture that tempts our kids to stumble and make bad choices; when they do, we're prone to criticize and ostracize and make it extremely hard for them to reconcile to the community. Can you name one ritual of reconciliation to welcome back our prodigals and celebrate their lost-and-found identity?

10

CRADLE SONG

THERE IS NO BETTER WAY to soothe a child's cries than with a lullaby. There is no better way to *save* Shabbat Shalom to the soul than through a swaddling in song. One of the greatest experiences of God's pleasure is the soul's tuning to the voice of its Creator.

> Now I lay me down to sleep,
> I pray the Lord my soul to keep.
> Thank you for another day,
> A chance to learn, a chance to play.

Everyone loves lullabies. Whether it's Luther's cradle song, or "Away in a Manger"; "Frére Jacques" ("Brother John"); the famous Brahms lullaby ("Lullaby and Goodnight"); the Welsh folk song "All through the Night"; or even "St. Judy's Comet," Paul Simon's lullaby written for his young son, these songs have become a staple of all world cultures to soothe the cries of a fussing infant, or to soothe the wounded souls of the oppressed.

The actual words of some lullabies aren't all that comforting. "Down will come baby, cradle and all," from "Rock-a-Bye, Baby," seems more disconcerting than settling. But the cradling arms and rocking-chair rhythms of the song create a safe, special place for an infant to rest.

Many of our most beloved nursery rhymes are plays on period fears, such as the rampage of Bloody Mary in "Mary, Mary, Quite Contrary," or the ravage of the Black Plague in "Ring around the Rosie." But the soothing melody of the song and lulling rhythm not only evoke endorphins but infuse a subliminal message that suggests, even during the most difficult times, we are safe within our parents' arms. Even more so in God's arms.

When we teach First Agers not just the stories but also the songs of our faith, we give them lullabies to live by, a life to sing about in all seasons and all weather, and a Shabbat Shalom way of Godplay. Who doesn't hum or whistle or even sing to chase away the blues? The haunting tunes of the spirituals, conceived in the African heartland but birthed on Southern plantations, tell stories of a people whose trust in God never wavered even in the most daunting conditions. A people or a church that sings together clings together, even under the harshest challenges. Even if we can't sing with our lips doesn't mean we don't have music in our souls and a song in our hearts.

The hymnbook we call the Psalms encoded ritual ways in which the Hebrew community dealt with hardships, tragedies, and mourning. But they were also songs of trust in the sovereignty and providence of God, and in the chosen identity of God's people. The church, throughout its history, has also known the power of song—from plainsongs to chants to folk songs to hymns to praise music. Throughout the centuries, the lyrics of joy and lament have been put to the music of daily doings.

Jesus' own life was born in song and finished in song. From the song sung by Mary while Jesus was still in the womb to his passionate singing of the Psalms on the cross, Jesus sang the "lullabies" of faith even with his last breath.

One of the most beautiful lullabies of our faith is Mary's "Magnificat."[1] In this song of praise, the mother of the unborn Savior sings of the promise of deliverance. Jesus' inaugural sermon for his mission, taken from the scroll of Isaiah, sounds like a song of hope to the poor and the outcast: "good news to the poor," "release to the captives," "recovering of sight to the blind"—all images from the lullaby his mother sang to him in the womb.[2] Mary's lullaby echoes the melody of God's song that began in the Garden and comforted God's people and gave them hope through the valleys. Jesus picked up the echo, on the cross, as he sang the words of Psalm 22: "The poor will eat and be satisfied; those who seek the Lord will praise him."[3] Jesus sang of promises kept: "He has done it!" The Messiah's voice, the voice of the Perfect Lamb, carried that lullaby home on God's "holy mountain" called Calvary.

Songs of faith are key sources of identity and formation. Within Mary's lullaby are echoes of the praises sung by those before her: the Song of the Sea; the Song of Deborah; songs by Miriam and Judith; the song sung by Samuel's mother, Hannah; and the song that would become the grace note of the celebration of Hanukkah. The first half of Mary's hymn is focused on what God has done in her life and how she has been blessed. The second half embraces what the future will hold for all of God's people—proclaiming that God's mighty arms and merciful acts will bring about a new age of hope and salvation for the world. In song, the celebration of both birth and rebirth through trial and tribulation soothe the listener while lamenting the circumstances of the world. In Mary's song, God comforts the world and lets the Lord's people know they are blessed and that they live in God's pleasure.

> My soul magnifies the Lord,
> and my spirit rejoices in God my Savior,
> for he has looked with favor on the lowliness of his
> servant.
> Surely, from now on all generations will call me blessed;
> for the Mighty One has done great things for me,
> and holy is his name.
> His mercy is for those who fear him
> from generation to generation.
> He has shown strength with his arm;
> he has scattered the proud in the thoughts of their
> hearts.
> He has brought down the powerful from their thrones,
> and lifted up the lowly;

he has filled the hungry with good things,
and sent the rich away empty.
He has helped his servant Israel,
in remembrance of his mercy,
according to the promise he made to our ancestors,
to Abraham and to his descendants forever.[4]

As with most lullabies, there are some dark and downside stanzas. The proud get knocked off their high horses, or fall from their pedestals. The powerful are scattered and brought low. The rich are sent away empty because "they already have their reward."[5] But the melodic leitmotif of Mary's lullaby confirms the identity of a people who see God as Savior, committed to the covenant, keeper of the promise made to Abraham and his ancestors.

There is good linguistic evidence to suggest that the term *lullaby* is derived from a Hebrew idiom—*lilith-aba* or "Lilith, begone!" Lilith is a demon from early Israelite literature who was believed to steal the souls of little children. "*Lilith-aba*" was part of the song sung over a child to protect the little one from evil. "*Lilith-aba*" became "lullaby."

So perhaps the first Hebrew lullabies were not just about putting children into a sleeping stupor, but keeping all of us alert to the approach of evil and aware of God's active saving and healing presence within the world.

Mary sang sweetly about the great gift she had received from God. But she also sang fiercely about the actions and changes that would come about because of the new work of God in the world—the birth of a Savior. Mary's first lullaby sung to baby Jesus was not designed to put him to sleep, but to "wake him up" to his mission in the world. The Messiah has come. Things will change. God's covenant is exercising the Good News, and God's promises are bringing great changes in the world.

The treasury of a people's memory is found in their songs. If we want to teach First Agers to play with God, to play in God's Garden, to "wake up" and go out in mission into the world for service in the "playing field of life," then we must teach them the songs of our faith, along with their narratives and metaphors. These are the songs that make the lips quiver and the spine shiver and turn acts of faith into acts of art.

The sound command of narrative identity awakens us to the pleasures of God and the joy that issues from living in God's pleasure. For Martin Luther, wine and song were of the same piece of cloth as learning and piety. "Waking up" and getting started on the road to discovery, listening and learning to recognize God's voice—this is the stuff of the First Age. The more stories and songs we teach First Agers, the surer and stronger they will hear God's voice over the din of the world: "Shabbat Shalom."

Sleep sweetly, child
The arms of Love
Enfold you.
Rest now,
Be still,
Relax and let Him hold you.
The day was His

And now His is the night.
And you,
Entirely His;
All will come right.
Entrust yourself to Him
Whose love
Has bound you.
Sleep sweetly child,
And let His love
Surround you.[6]

PART III

Second Age (30–60)
Real Player: Rocking and Real-ing

11

DANCING WITH THE STARS

A CHILD'S SANDBOX is the university of play. Second Age disciples never get done learning, exploring, playing, or singing, but now they must learn to play with God in a much bigger sandbox. The Second Age is a time of maturing, anointing, and commissioning. In our faith, it's a time when we go beyond our baptism, and faith "comes of age." The Second Age used to begin with a celebration called *confirmation* or *conversion*. Camp meetings and revivals were the nineteenth-century Protestant equivalent of the Jewish bar or bat mitzvah. Today, we have lost these coming-of-age initiations, not to mention initiatives.

In the first century, the Second Age began somewhere around the age of twelve and lasted until about thirty. In the twenty-first century, the Second Age begins more or less around thirty. Of course, for some it begins earlier, for some later. For some, the personal initiative to follow Jesus comes early. But while in the First Age we are nurtured within a community of faith, in the Second Age, we become full members of that community as Truth makers, Beauty stakers, and Goodness sakers.

Whereas a First Ager discovers his or her song and learns to sing it in the world, a Second Ager learns to dance with a partner and to make music within a symphony of voices. To dance and play through life becomes the challenge of the Second Age disciple. For the First Ager, play comes easily; in the Second Age, getting "real" is culturally interpreted to mean putting play behind and "getting serious" about work, career, family, future. Some career coaches encourage *everyone* to start a "side business" or "side hustle," no matter their primary job or profession.[1]

> *He [Yahweh] will exult with joy over you,*
> *he will renew you by his love;*
> *he will dance with shouts of joy for you*
> *as on a day of festival.*
>
> ZEPHANIAH 3:17, JB

But this is where we get lost—not "lost in wonder, love, and praise," but lost in work and workaholism. We impoverish our lives in the Second Age with a surfeit of seriousness. A job or business is more than an activity of work that generates income and employment. A job or business should be a form of play that pursues God's pleasures of learning and growing—of intellectual stimulation, imaginative activity, risk-taking innovation, but-what-if creativity (*butwhatifer* is another word for "Godplayer").

There are lots of good reasons to start up a business or to enter a profession or to take a job. Making money isn't one of them. Doing something that brings us pleasure is the best of them. Doing something that serves humanity in the service of God is unbeatable. Godplayers don't open up a coffee shop to get rich. They open up a coffee shop because it's fun and serves the common good by providing a "third space" commons.[2]

A work mind-set creates Macy's inch-thick rulebook. A play mind-set creates Nordstrom's two-sentence strange attractor: (1) Use good judgment in all situations; (2) there are no additional rules.[3] Self-worth is not best measured by standards of work or career, but by stories of enjoyment and pleasure. Work is when we struggle to solve problems; play is when we pleasure in puzzles and problem solving.

Pablo Picasso, one of the most prolific artists who ever lived, warned of what happens when you try to "get a life" through your work: "You put more of yourself into your work, until one day, you never know exactly which day, it happens—you *are* your work. The passions that motivate you may change, but it is your work in life that is the ultimate seduction."[4] The human species is the apex of God's creation, but we ape the apes when it comes to work. Or to be more precise, as revealed by the triumvirate of great-ape researchers—Jane Goodall (chimpanzees), Dian Fossey (mountain gorillas), and Biruté Mary Galdikas (orangutans)— we could learn some things from these creatures about taking delight in life, not just in labor.

———————— ◇ ————————

If you want to build a ship, don't herd people together to collect wood and don't assign them tasks and work, but rather teach them to long for the endless immensity of the sea.

ANTOINE DE SAINT-EXUPÉRY

John Locke, perhaps the greatest philosopher of the Enlightenment, asserted that "labour for labour's sake is against nature."[5] He joined many others in believing that there would be no *work* in heaven. Daniel Pink, one of the more influential management thinkers alive today, takes the Peter Principle one step further to the "Peter-Out Principle." The Peter Principle holds that workers rise in the workplace to their level of incompetence, and then stall out.[6] Pink's Peter-Out Principle holds that people rise in the workplace to their level of displeasure, "until they stop having fun."[7]

◇

Life, as it is called, is for most of us one long postponement.

HENRY MILLER

We have been so complicit in this conspiracy of work that we have even made Jesus into a *worker* and God's mission into *work*. We have translated the Greek word *tekton* as "carpenter," when it could just as easily refer to an *artisan* known for the art of poetry, the composer of songs, the painter of pictures, or most likely, the carver of stone. The Greek word *sunergei* we have translated as "work," as in "All things work [*sunergei*] together for good for those who love God"[8] and "They went forth, and preached everywhere, while the Lord worked [*sunergei*] with them."[9] But actually, "all things synergize for good" and "the Lord synergized with them" convey much better the actual Greek meaning. God is the ultimate synergizer, not worker. Maybe our inability to comprehend the power of prayer is due in part to our making prayer more work than synergy.

For Thomas Aquinas, considered the church's greatest theologian and philosopher, synergy and prudence were different ways of talking about the same thing. *Prudentia* (prudence) was a contraction of *providentia* (providence). In other words, prudence is not caution at work, but synergy at play—our participation in God's providence. We are not puppets at the end of some divinely pulled string, but stringed instruments and musical collaborators in the orchestra of creation.[10]

The sacred is not found in work as much as it is in play. In a work paradigm, we go through life learning lessons. In a play paradigm, we go through life ripening our souls. In a work paradigm, we acquire a worldview. In a play paradigm, we author a life story.[11] In a work paradigm, we aim to please God. In a play paradigm, we savor God's pleasure. In a work paradigm, we "do good." In a play paradigm, we "be God's." In a work paradigm, we hold on to control. In a play paradigm, we live in the flow.

> *When I pray, coincidences happen; when I do not pray, they do not happen.*
>
> ARCHBISHOP OF CANTERBURY WILLIAM TEMPLE

The well-played life can be realized in every moment of every day—in our jobs, our family lives, our playgrounds, playlists, playdates, playcreation. God's Kingdom is best seen as a *play*dom. In fact, when work becomes play, we don't know we're working at all, only playing.

Of course, not everyone's vocation and vacation can be one and the same. Or as poet Robert Frost expressed his goal in life: "My object in living is to unite / My avocation and my vocation / As my two eyes make one in sight."[12] But we can even play when we're doing drudgery. For example, cleaning, dusting, fixing up can be play when we use the time to reconnect with the stories that provenance what we are cleaning. This presupposes that what we allow into our personal space is not stuff, but stories, stories that are vitalizing and soul-making.

There are few people I respect more than day laborers and factory workers. In the summer of my senior year of high school, I worked a five-to-five, six-day shift at a Coleco plant in Mayfield, New York. My job was to put a sheet of plastic into a hot oven, where it was molded into the form of a backyard kiddie wading pool. Then I sawed off the excess plastic, stacked the pools, and salvaged the discarded trim on the floor to be melted down and recycled into new sheets of plastic. It was a brutal job: hot, boring, high-pressure, with increasing demands to go faster and make bigger stacks of swimming pools. For me it was a summer job, but for some of the guys, it was where they would spend the rest of their lives.

What made life in the plant bearable was turning the work into play. Some guys would hang pictures of their wives and girlfriends near the ovens and sing to the plastic slabs as if they were lovers. Others would play practical jokes on colleagues, creating a party atmosphere even under the watchful glances of the supervisors. Games of one kind or another were always being played, and every person who punched in was a gossip columnist. Pub time after work was when the "dirt" was shared and the stories circulated in community. Swearing was raised to the level of art form, and I learned to hear the words not as vulgarity but as personality and humanity breaking through the concrete pavement of commodification. I myself got a reputation for having a vile and dirty mouth when, in a moment of pious rebuke to the swearing, I replaced "G** dammit" with "America dammit." Before I had ever read Rousseau, that was the moment I discovered that everyone has two religions: a faith religion and a civil religion.

My senior summer was when I learned that we all hug the hope of a better life. The rich play the stock market. The poor play the lottery. This was also the summer that gave a nasty chop to my naive optimism about human nature and life. The world is not benign. Things don't always work out, and the universe does not always support our backbreaking industry or best intentions. Some of the best had the worst happen to them. But the grinding life of *odtaa* ("one d*** thing after another") could become a girding, girdling life of one *dawn* thing after another when it is reframed as creative play: "Let there be . . ."

This was also the summer when I resolved in my heart that if I ever returned to faith (I deconverted from Christianity at seventeen and became an atheist), it would not be a religion for church Pharisees or a religion for the PhD crowd, but a "get real" religion for these Coleco blue-collars.

However menial Paul's job of tent making, doing God's mission in the world is never *work* when you are living in God's pleasure. *Real* disciples play. *Real* disciples dance. *Real* disciples don't just learn to schedule playtimes, but practice playing in every field of life. Adults who leave their childlikeness behind don't get real, they get real old.

Doing God's mission in the world is not work when you are living in the pleasure of God. Let's face it. We are not a Sabbath people. We have made sabbathing into a self-help manual instead of a Spirit-liberating song. But only when we live a Sabbath life filled with the joy of being "in the service" can we begin to really "get real" in our discipleship.

Second Age disciples take with them their First Age wonders and chronicles. They never forget how to sing their songs, or to listen for God's voice in all of creation, or to "eat what is good and . . . delight yourself in abundance."[13] But most of all, Second Agers never forget to play at life and live in the pleasure of God.

There is nothing wrong with working hard and doing well. But what we call *work* is best done as Godplay and to the pleasure of God. Maybe this is one of the reasons that Martin Luther, known for his love of food, drink, and friends, as well as spending time with his treasured Katharina, so viciously attacked the biblical book of James. In several sermons, Luther insisted that *love* trumps *law*. Love issues from faith, so that the one who loves bears the fruit of the Spirit and lives in the joy of the Lord. For Luther, God's anointing was a license to laugh a lot, love a lot, dance a lot, sing a lot, play a lot, and celebrate life in all its seasons. Such is the Kingdom of God.

◇

The only chance an animal has of growing old is within a group.

MIDAS DEKKERS

Some people confuse growing older and more mature and deeper in their discipleship with a "hardening of the categories" and "hardening of the oughteries."[14] In the former, positions of power delude us into thinking that our categories are hard-and-fast—and even ultimate—understandings of truth that protect us from those who would make visible the dusty layers of fossilized thinking and musty assumptions that have accumulated in our minds over the years. In the latter, we mistake "oughts" for *wisdom*, and thus a naughty-oughty, nit-picking, pointy finger replaces an arm-waving cheer or an encouraging squeeze on the shoulder.

This is why the modern world was so addicted to dispute, and in many ways became a culture of complaint. Academic circles privileged the negative. "Critical studies" ensured that the negative always won. You made a scholarly reputation not by cheering someone else's thesis, but by taking down the giants and geniuses as if they were cretins. This is like stomping on someone's kneecaps while standing on their shoulders.

Criticism is the arena of workers, not players. In fact, R. P. Blackmur defines criticism as "the formal discourse of an amateur."[15] The Psalms begin with a warning about "management by objection" when it refers to "sitting in the seat of the scornful."[16] Criticism occurs from a seated position, often high in the bleachers.[17] Players stand out; they stand in the gaps. A playing posture is one of standing up and running for standards of virtue and truth.

It is not the "oughts" of Christ that constrain us, Paul said, but the "love of Christ constrains us."[18] When work flows from faith and is done for the love of God, it feels joyful and not direful, liberating and not limiting. Rather than "faith without works is dead,"[19] Martin Luther maintained that "works without faith is dead," after reading Romans 3:28 in 1517. It was this insight that sparked the Reformation.

Almost five hundred years later, it's time for a post-Reformation church to take Luther one step further: *"Faith without play is dead."*[20] In the words of Fanny Crosby's most popular hymn, "This is my story, this is my song, praising my Savior all the day long."[21] This is why humans were created: to compose a narrative of delight in and to dance before God. No one can be happy unless their "house not made with hands" is happy in God and, as Mary's Magnificat would put it, "magnifies the Lord," reflecting back to the Creator the holiness of the Lord's light.

Imagine two dancers in a spotlight, their motions flowing, their steps in sync, bathed in a halo of light. Beauty, goodness, truth—this is what life with God is designed to be.

In our dance with the divine, only one is leading. Christ, the Lord of the Dance, is most joyful of all when we are dancing in sync with the symphony of Creation's Conductor. A Jewish exposition of the Song of Songs declares that, in the next age, God will lead the dance among the righteous.[22] No wonder the Hebrew people love to dance in worship and praise. In fact, Saul danced so hard with Samuel's prophets that he passed out for hours.[23] David danced and led a dance processional.[24] What was Hebrew worship without dance? To burst forth in praise to God was to dance.

Dancing requires embodiment. Embodied worship changes how we feel. (We cannot worship God with a cold and hard heart and still dance.) And it changes how we experience others. When we dance together, we share a mutuality and reciprocity of intimacy that involves every part of our being. When we worship solo, we worship self. When we worship "in the midst," whether alone or with a partner, we dance the Lord's dance.

In the case of multiple meanings of words, we have often chosen to translate a word from Greek into one in English that supports a meaning we favor. However, undeniably, the word *dance* appears in the Old Testament, in various forms, at least forty times. The Hebrew word for "feast," for example, *chagag*, is the word for celebrating in sacred dance, just as the verb *chuwl* ("to twirl in a circle dance") refers to dancing in praise before the Lord. "O Worship the Lord in the beauty of holiness. . . . Dance before him." Hebrew feasts were times of joy, celebration, and dances of praise with voice and instruments.

> *We then that are strong ought to bear the infirmities of the weak, and not to please ourselves.*
>
> PAUL THE APOSTLE

When we celebrate the Lord, when we celebrate life, God does not want us to sit motionless and solemn as if at a funeral, but to celebrate and dance, because every time of feasting is a remembrance of the sacred wedding feast that celebrates our blessed covenant with the Lord. The Lord of the Dance invites us to *sing* our lives and *dance* with the divine. Holiness is a dance of joy, and a time of *playing* in God's presence. The Song of Songs is one of the least-quoted Scriptures in our churches, and yet it is one of the most joyful of our Sabbath Scriptures, celebrating the wedding feast that is a metaphor of our joyful covenant with God and with one another, a covenant of holistic love that is not just *eros* or *phileo*, but deeply and encompassingly *agape*.

Holiness is not about getting better at keeping God's commandments. Holiness is about getting better at enjoying God, paying attention to God (which is really what the term *commandments* means, but that's another story), and reveling in God's pleasure (to borrow from Eric Liddell in *Chariots of Fire*).[25] The respiration of the Christian life is quite simple: When we run toward God, we inhale happiness and exhale holiness with the air we breathe.[26] In this way, the moral climate of the world is cleansed.

Those who desire holiness must learn and relearn to play with God. God-pleasing and Godplaying replace goal seeking and vision casting. Does your church life revolve around goals? Do you go through a vision-casting process every five years? Or do you seek to be quick to fall on your knees and spring fast on your feet to *be* the people of God in every walk of life? Participation in God's nature is the true *goal* of human life.

Love is not work. Love is play . . . that requires a lot of practice. Now replace the word *love* with *God* in that sentence (because God is Love)[27] . . . and there you have this book in a nutshell. We acquire the skill of playing the violin by playing it. We become players by playing. Acquiring any virtue or deepening faith or loving someone is like acquiring any skill: it requires practice.

In the Second Age, to dance with a partner is like learning the tango or the salsa.[28] Sometimes we misstep, sometimes we use the wrong foot, but we keep on dancing. It helps if we can laugh at our mistakes, if we can catch one another when we stumble, if we can slow up sometimes and practice our moves. If our lives are a dance of praise to God, we will learn to live in God's pleasure.

Of course, learning to dance with others can be hard. Relationships are not easy. We not only have to practice our steps and our posture but must practice relaxing in someone else's arms and letting someone else lead, all the while listening to the music. When we dance with Jesus, we have to learn to let go of trying to control the way the dance will go and learn to follow. A dance with a partner is like a yoke. We have freedom of movement, but we must stay in sync with our partner, or we will not create that graceful and beautiful symmetry that our lives can be.

> *God is a comedian playing to an audience too afraid to laugh.*
>
> VOLTAIRE

And *symmetry* is the ultimate success. A work ethic defines opportunity in terms of "Will it pay?" or "Will it please people?" A play ethic asks, "Will it set my soul to dancing?" or "Will it make me a nobler human being?" or "Will it reveal to the world the goodness and glory of God?" The work ethic leads to valued collections. The play ethic leads to valued connections. The work ethic defines success in life in terms of increasing status. In the play ethic, advancement in life consists of increasing stature and intimacy . . . with God.

Giuseppe Verdi, one of the most commercially successful composers of the nineteenth century, had only one measure of success for his operas: Did they please the crowd? "The one and only barometer of success is the box office."[29] In

Godplay, there is only one scorecard: the symmetry of the dance.

Mihaly Csikszentmihalyi, the world's leading scholar of creativity, tells this story:

> I used to know an old man in one of the decrepit suburbs of Naples who made a precarious living out of a ramshackle antique store his family had owned for generations. One morning a prosperous-looking American lady walked into the store, and after looking around for a while, asked the price of a pair of baroque wooden *putti*, those chubby little cherubs so dear to Neapolitan craftsmen of a few centuries ago. . . . Signor Orsini, the owner, quoted an exorbitant price. The woman took out her folder of traveler's checks, ready to pay for the dubious artifacts. I held my breath, glad for the unexpected windfall about to reach my friend. But I didn't know Signor Orsini well enough. He turned purple and with barely contained agitation escorted the customer out of the store: "No, no, *signora*, I am sorry but I cannot sell you those angels. . . . I cannot make business with you. You understand?" After the tourist finally left, he calmed down and explained: "If I were starving, I would have taken her money. But since I am not, why should I make a deal that isn't any fun? I enjoy the clash of wits involved in bargaining, when two persons try to outdo each other with ruses and with eloquence. She didn't even

flinch. She didn't know any better. She didn't pay me the respect of assuming that I was going to try to take advantage of her. If I had sold those pieces to that woman at that ridiculous price, I would have felt cheated."[30]

Here is someone for whom work was not an end in itself nor a means to money, but a means to the meaning of delight in connection and the dance of play.

Besides haggling over prices, playfulness can take many forms . . . from running to walking, from leaping to skipping, from dancing to plodding. William Carey, the "father of modern missions," started his mission to India with no money, no support, and no discernible talent. "I can plod," he said. "Plodding" may have summed up the full range of his assets, but he led thousands to Christ.

Sometimes, playing is plodding. Sometimes, playing is blundering. I can blunder into bathos in the blink of an eye. And bathos is but one step removed from chaos. I've pursued many projects that didn't pan out. Many glass slippers refused to fit; many big ideas blundered. But I continue to stay in the game with God.

———————— ◇ ————————

God respects me when I work, but He loves me when I sing.

RABINDRANATH TAGORE

12

ROCK, PAPER, SCISSORS

A DISCIPLE OF JESUS who never disciples another is like a mariner who has never gone to sea or an explorer who never leaves home. The Second Age is the heartland of discipling others and being discipled.

It is also the age when we are most vulnerable to breakdowns and burnouts from workaholism and its attendants— the pride of life, the lust of the eye, and the love of things that perish. Each age has its devils, against which we must be on guard. Busied out of play and bustled out of pleasure bedevils the Second Age, robbing life of its joy and delight. All fall. But those on their high horses, at the height of personal power and prosperity, with noses high in the air, fall furthest and fastest, partly because they can't see the pitfalls and potholes.

Of course, every age needs fresh understandings of how Jesus changes lives, but Second Agers are especially needy. Not only are those of the Second Age *working* too hard at life, drained dry by success-driven striving instead of flush with relational pleasures; they are also not finding ways to *connect* their faith with the church in ways that don't get bogged down in stock religion or bureaucratic gridlock. This is also the age when we can get so busy building our careers, providing for our families, paying off educational debts, taking care of parents, and saving for the future that we can be as dense to things of the Spirit as Balaam, whose ass saw the angel before he did.

If we are to play our lives with God, especially in a gaming culture, then perhaps the best way to portray the satisfactions of Christ over the tumult of our lives is in the form of a game, complete with hand motions. You might call this gestural game *embodied evangelism*—or if you will, *graphic theology* (as in graphic novels).

Lately, one of my favorite things to do with audiences is to ask my DJ (digital jockey) to Google live on the screen, "Why are Christians so . . ." and see what pops up. Because Google is totally search dependent, the results are always unpredictable, but there is one thing 99 percent predictable: The key words are almost always negative. If you type in, "Why are Christians so *a*," you might find words such as *annoying* and *arrogant* heading the list. Type in, "Why are Christians so *b*," and you get *brainwashed* and *bigoted*. Try it with the letter *c* and you get "unlike Christ." The list goes on as long as the alphabet. Try it yourself.

Nothing tells the story faster of how the world today views Christians and what it means to live out our faith in the world. From the ground up, Christians appear not as people illuminating Christ, the most majestic character the world has ever seen, but as rigid, sad, snappy, judgmental, joyless people. How then do we take the Good News of Christ's saving power to a world that looks at us as harbingers of hate and gloom?

In one of the other books I'm writing now, I asked myself that very question. How do you explain to people today that to follow Jesus is to be alive twice—with the second time so much better than the first? What I came up with was a new way to explain the Good News by engaging people in Godplay through a game.

The game is one that may be familiar to you. It is played all over the world and is passed on virally from generation to generation. I recently tried playing the game in Surabaya, Indonesia, and the Indonesians knew it as well. The game is called "Rock, Paper, Scissors" (RPS).

Without historical creeds, apologetic treatises, doctrinal statements, or step-by-step laws, RPS uses a combination of gestures, accessible to all generations and cultures, to show the dynamic interaction between sin and separation, the freedom to write our own stories, and Jesus' power of salvation. RPS shows what we can do to break harmful cycles in our lives and how to embrace the grace of God. In a culture that is game riveted, gesture filled, and metaphor savvy, RPS uses a method of "nudge" evangelism to explain how our lives can get sliced and diced by sin and written over by shame, selfishness, and separation.[1] By showing the ways we try to hide and cover ourselves from God's presence and try to write Jesus out of our lives, RPS invites those inside and outside the fold to embrace the dance of faith through which Christ's power can break addictive cycles and overcome all obstacles.

Rock, Paper, Scissors is, in a sense, a Game of Life. Like all good games, it must be difficult enough so that players feel challenged, but not so difficult that they give up in frustration. It is a simple and EPIC (experiential, participatory, image-rich, connective) way to spread the Good News to a twenty-first-century culture in which doctrinal Christianity is difficult to understand or relate to, but an awareness of sovereignty, sin, and salvation is more important than ever.

In the traditional RPS game, each gesture has a meaning, a function, and a consequence. Scissors cuts Paper; Paper covers Rock; and Rock breaks Scissors. Sin is our Scissors. Our lives (our stories) are Paper. Jesus is the Rock, the Rock of Ages. Our salvation is set in stone. Jesus is a rock solid reality. The most important journey we make in life is the journey from sin to salvation, the journey of Paper from Scissors to Rock.

Every parent has the same mantra: "Never run with scissors!" Scissors are dangerous weapons. They are strong, sharp, and powerfully hinged. When using only one part, they jab and stab. But when hinged together, they become even more powerful.

The nature of sin is not the violation of a moral code, but the tearing of a relationship. Sin slices and dices our lives into shreds, turning us into mere fragments of our whole selves, with deep bruises on our souls. The Scissors of sin *separate*, *infiltrate*, and *negate* our true selves and stories, leaving us dysfunctional and deaf, no longer on speaking terms with the universe. When Scissors cut into the stories of our lives, they can cut out everything good and beautiful that we know to be true about ourselves.

Scissors cut Paper. God created in us the power to *construct*, and we have used our power to construct Scissors. God does not use those Scissors to shred our lives. We do that all on our own. Through our desire to craft ourselves into the image we want, instead of the one God made us to be, we have become People of the Scissors. In our hands, scissoring can run rampant and amuck. Soon we find that the Scissors are stronger than we are; and like Edward Scissorhands, our Scissors become a cyborg for our hands in the world. When that happens, we not only find our own lives shredded, but we begin to shred the lives of others as well.

In 1518, Martin Luther noted that sinners are not loved because they are attractive; they are attractive because they are loved. It's an important distinction. Conditional love says, "I love you *because* you have worked so hard and done everything perfectly." It is a very different kind of love that says, "I love you *even though* you have been cut down, cut off, cut up, and have cut me out."

The symbol of the Scissors is a fist with two fingers extended. The fingers of accusation are like the forked tongue that points aggressively and defiantly to others, to our lives, and to God.

> *Jesus didn't come just to save us from problems we have, but from the problem we are.*
> MYRON S. AUGSBURGER

But Paper, too, can be double sided. Our lives can be turned upward to write the story of Jesus, or they can face down to write another story. They can be a living letter or a dead letter, which is a dead end. Although there are no clean slates in life, God created us with a free will, a tabula rasa ("blank page") on which we get to write the story of our lives. We are born to continue writing the Jesus story, and we can use our Paper to either pick up or cover up the Rock of Ages. When we pick up the Rock and allow God's covenant to be written in our hearts,[2] our lives glow as the Son, as icons of Christ. Too often, though, we hoard that Paper to ourselves and cover up the divine image in ourselves with our own makeup and others' makeovers. Whether out of guilt or fear or pride or defiance, we scissor our page out of God's Book of Life and start writing our own book. We try to do life on our own.

The Cherokee tribe of Native Americans had a special name for the pages on which the white man scribbled and then spoke by looking at the inky squiggles on white paper: *talking leaves*. Each one of us is a "talking leaf," an organic image of God, created by the Rock of Ages. Just as no two leaves are the same, no two slips of Paper are the same. Each one of us is a "fifth Gospel." There are the Gospels of Matthew, Mark, Luke, John . . . and you. We each continue the Jesus story on the pages of our own lives as the gospel becomes "my gospel" and then "our gospel" until it finally becomes a special edition "fifth Gospel," even perhaps a "third Testament"—the gospel translated into our lives and written between the lines on the pages of Scripture.

The story of "talking leaves" is the story of the Garden. What began as a page out of a beautiful story of a relationship between the divine and the human has become our "fig leaf" and our "tower of Babel." We use our Paper to declare our independence from God. We use our Paper to hide from

God. Perhaps we think the pages of our lives are so inked from wrong choices, or so jaggedly cut and sliced by sin, that God would not want to write any story on them. We become ashamed of our stories. So we shut the cover on our pages and shield our lives from God.

Toddlers think that if they turn their backs, we can't see what they are doing. We do much the same when we hide our lives, our stories, from God. Soon, when we look in the mirror, instead of seeing a reflection of God's beautiful image, we see our own crossed-out, cut-down image. We close our pages even tighter. We even delude ourselves that we are hiding our stories and blocking God's face from our lives. But we underestimate the steadfast mercy and amazing, encompassing grace of God.

Paper covers Rock. We may cover up God's image in our lives and erase Jesus' face from our stories, but in so doing we allow sin to cut us down to "snafu size" (situation normal, all fouled up) and tear us to pieces. When our shame and our guilt make us hide from God, we start the cycle all over again. Only when we release the Rock to triumph over Scissors can our stories be freed to become chapters in the Greatest Story Ever Told.

The symbol for Paper is a flat, extended hand. Ever hear the saying, "talk to the hand"? The hand that covers the Rock doesn't reach out in love, but signals separation. As long as we detach ourselves from God and tell God to "talk to the hand," we cannot break the cycle of separation and sin. Only Jesus can break that cycle. When we allow Jesus to write his life on our pages—unfettered, unedited, uncovered—we begin to see ourselves reappear as Jesus breaks the grip of the Scissors and the beauty of his character becomes evident once again on the pages of our lives.

Rock breaks Scissors. Jesus is the Living Rock, the Rock of Ages, and the Rock of our Salvation. He is a stumbling stone to those running with Scissors, and the cornerstone that breaks their hinges and renders them useless. Rock dulls Scissors (sin) and leaves it powerless to damage our stories. The symbol of the Rock is a fist—a hand that is strong and opens up to take and grasp Paper. When we allow our Paper to be picked up by the Rock, we allow the power of the Rock to smash even those besetting sins that hold us in bondage.

Like the Phantom of the Opera, we wear masks to shield ourselves from ourselves, not just from God. We detest the image we have made of ourselves, and we judge ourselves unlovable. Before we know it, the unlovable become the unloving. When we dare to unmask before God, we allow the Solid Rock of grace to smash those mirrors to smithereens and replace them with the true image of Christ. We can now show our true face to the world, confident that the world will see Jesus in us.

The beauty of the Rock is that the Rock becomes our new identity, the one that God intended for us. Like Peter, who is renamed Petros—or Rocky—by Jesus, we each become a Rocky, the image of Christ imparted to us and implanted within our own stories as God's story becomes ours. Paul picks up this "rock" image and portrays every member of the church as specially designed, Master-Architect-signed, living stones, which fit together to make strong and beautiful the walls of the Lord's house, a temple not made with hands.[3]

The prayer that breaks the Scissors of sin and creates the image of Christ the Solid Rock in us can be said in multiple ways, but it may be best expressed in the simple prayer used in ancient baptismal liturgies: "Another Christ sent into the world." When we stop *im*personating and start personating Christ, we inhabit the name we've inherited—"little Christs" (*Christ-ians*) sent into the world for ministry and mission, steadfast in faith, passionate in love, imperishable in hope.

Rock, Paper, Scissors is a children's game with adult apps. It is a story of the Second Age, a time fraught with busyness, loneliness, confusion, and despair. As the song "Lord of the Dance" tells us, "It's hard to dance with the devil on your back."[4] Second Agers need to open themselves to the redeeming Rhythm of the Rock, so that they can dance again with the Lord of the Dance.

In *The Sound of Music*, Mother Superior turns Maria away from the convent. She tells Maria she must not use the convent as an excuse to hide from love and life. In the Second Age, "hiding places" abound. For some, it is the church and its buildings and grounds. For others, religion and legalities. For still others, it is work or shopping or eating or television. All these are Second Age addictions or hiding places.

All hiding places separate us from God and from one another, causing us to stop dancing. God created us to live in relationship—to God, to one another, to Christ, to creation. When those relationships are dropped or turned into principles, we stop dancing. And when we stop dancing, we stop being human and turn into something else, something subhuman.

In any wedding ceremony, there are vows. But vows are made to a person, not to a proposition—or to "irrefutable laws" or "foundational principles." Propositions end up nailed on doors and posted on blogs. Vows end up carrying for-better-or-worse bedpans and keeping vigils at deathbeds.

The game Rock, Paper, Scissors makes us face the "games" we play with God to avoid getting real in our joy. The true meaning of living a well-played life is making the Dance of the Trinity our own dance. When we get faith formidable, we take off our work boots and put on our dancing shoes. Then we begin to rock and roll the world.

13

SHAKE, RATTLE, AND ROLL

In *FLIGHT*, the 2012 film for which Denzel Washington was nominated for an Academy Award as best actor, he plays a pilot named "Whip" Whitaker, who masterfully lands a doomed plane, saving many people aboard. While being celebrated for his miraculous feat, Whip realizes that his own life is a "crash landing," that he is far from being saved and far from being alive. The real miracle of life for Whip becomes the healing that later allows him to walk away healthy, happy, and whole. Life's pleasures did not come from a lofty level of professional skill and cocky self-assurance, but from the depth of his relationships. The well-played life is not about never falling. It is about how we roll when we crash, how we walk away after we get up, and whom we walk away with.

Part of rocking and real-ing for a Second Ager is admitting we all wobble. To say something is not to get everything right. The number one rule of dancers is that if you trip or tumble, you keep dancing—and don't stop dancing until you get to the end of the dance. As we journey down the Pilgrim Road, we can't get discouraged when we go flat or fall flat. Instead, we get up, dust ourselves off, and keep going on our way.

The best will fail the most. George Washington lost more battles than he won. Thomas Edison scrapped more "great ideas" than he ever saw come to fruition. Jesus even gave his disciples a rite of failing: "Shake off the dust."[1] Not everyone will listen to the Good News, or if they do, not everyone will hear it as good news. If we sow seeds, not every seed will take. If we invite someone to dance, not everyone will take our hands. But if our dancing partner is Jesus, we don't need to worry about rejection. We just need to maintain our poise, practice our posture, learn our steps, stay in sync with the music, and enjoy the dance. No matter how many times we fall or step on toes, Jesus calls us to get back up and keep stepping out. *Real* disciples know not just how to rock, but how to roll—how to shake off the dust and keep on dancing.

Besides, it's not our bailiwick to decide success or failure. We never know how God will use our rocking and real-ing. Aubrey Beardsley (one of the greatest illustrators of history) provided the pictures for Oscar Wilde's *Salome*, published in 1894. Most reviewers ignored Beardsley's contributions, and those that commented on his work were not complimentary. Today, however, more people know the drawings than the book.

◇

Let us seek as they seek who must find, and find as they find who must go on seeking.

AUGUSTINE

The missionary evangelist E. Stanley Jones thought his book on Mahatma Gandhi was a dud. His initial reluctance to write about his friendship with Gandhi, suspecting that no one would be interested, seemed vindicated by the sales. But it was this book, picked up by Martin Luther King Jr. in the library stacks of Boston University School of Theology when he was working on his doctorate, that convinced King that the nonviolent resistance of *satyagraha* ("soul force") was a practical political strategy that could be adopted and adapted in the civil rights struggle.

Dancers also know another little secret for preventing slippage: *rosin*. Powdered rosin is a white substance made from the sticky sap of trees (and used in making lacquers and pitch). Dancers rub powdered rosin on the soles of their shoes to gain traction so they don't slip on the shiny, slick floors, whether in dance halls or boardrooms.

Disciples who have maximum traction in their lives don't rattle easily. Instead, they have a "rattling good time" dancing with more and more powerful steps. Traction makes it easier to take risks and stay the course. The "stickiness" of those stories learned in childhood can't be shaken, no matter how stirred life becomes.

Second Agers are prone to get stuck on "by the sweat of your brow you shall eat bread," rather than "my God shall supply all your need according to his riches in glory."[2] Even when life is most dense with duties and thick with responsibilities, God wants to have a rattling good time with us. Not *rattle* in the sense of "rattling on," which is to gossip about a person. Not *rattle* in the sense of "rattling someone's cage," which is to unnerve a person. Not *rattle* in the sense of "rattling the mind," which is to shake someone to the point of losing composure. To have a "rattling good time" with God is to receive God's gifts of mountaintops—to be blown away by the energy and excitement of life's peak moments.

In a work paradigm, when we get to adulthood, we cast off the "rattle" and settle into the "hum"—the blasé, the bland, the everyday ennui of life. The truth is . . . getting *real* with God, when we rock and roll with the Spirit, shakes us out of our complacencies and stirs in us new dreams and desires to do more than rattle a few chains in the world, even to rock the very bowels of the earth in Jesus' name.

Anything good in life puts *risk* into play. In fact, recent scientific studies have concluded that humans and organizations endure and mature, not *in spite* of their willingness to take risks, but *because* of their risk taking.[3] For safety's sake and security needs, we want to make the next moment like the one before it. Hence, the power of the status quo, the challenge of change, and the need to defuse our deep-seated squeamishness about risking anything at all. Ironically, in the risk-averse world of the church, we play it safe with our mission and fast and loose with our inheritance. The current condition of the church is a stark portrayal of what safety-first living does to the soul.

Risk is a choice, but a difficult one to make in the look-before-you-leap world of the Second Age. Today, however, a different paradigm is at work—or more precisely, at play—in our culture. Bungee jumping, competitive skateboarding, heli-skiing, high-risk-tolerant First Agers are usurping the word *extreme* from the timid ("Don't get too close to the edge, honey") and claiming it as their own ("Hey, dude, watch *this* . . .").

The Spirit's warning to the church of Laodicea—"Because you are . . . neither cold nor hot, I will spew you out of my mouth"[4]—validates a life lived as far away as possible from a "safe-and-secure-from-all-alarms" center.[5] When there is no indication that we are up and about and active at the edges, pushing the envelope, taking risks, playing with fire and water, the prognosis of a healthy future is doubtful.

There is an incredible moment in the book of Exodus, when the children of Israel are poised on the banks of the Red Sea. Hearing the thunder of Pharaoh's approaching chariots, the people start clamoring to God for help. When Moses adds his voice to their prayers, he gets a rough answer from God: "Why do you cry to me? Tell the people of Israel to go forward."[6] Or to put it more bluntly, *Stop praying and get moving!*

Jesus does not want his followers, of whatever age, to hunker down and duck their heads. Disciples are not called to avoid high-stakes risks and genuine challenges. A disciple of Jesus operates in the world of risk. Jesus placed himself in the firing line of history. Sometimes he calls us to place ourselves in the firing line of history as well.

The parable of the talents is less about "using our talents wisely" than it is about risking everything for the Master's Kingdom. The hundredfold increase of "talents" for those servants who risked everything isn't a lesson in wise money management. Instead, it is a call to step out beyond the safe avenues, the conventional adventures, with faith that putting everything in the hands of God is the best investment we can make. Only by giving everything over, only by placing ultimate control beyond our short reach, only by putting everything into play, do we find the *joy* that Jesus' parable promises.

Too many mistakenly think of the church as a "safe haven," a "sanctuary" away from the dangers and risks of the world. Instead, the church is where disciples receive the "talents," the gifts of faith and forgiveness, grace and love, that enable them to become risk takers and daredevils in the eyes of the rest of the world.

Who but Christ's disciples can have the audacity to offer the miracle of redemption to everyone who asks for it?

What other community of faith can risk extending love and hope to a broken world, with the knowledge that they cannot fail, for Christ has already triumphed?

The true definition of a sanctuary is not a place that is safe from risks. A true sanctuary is a place where it is safe to *take* risks. When did the church become such a "risk-free-at-any-cost" zone? Where does Jesus call his disciples to follow him and say he will lead them into a "risk-free-at-any-cost" life?

For the Christian, risk-taking is a given, stepping on toes is a lifestyle, and trespassing is an occupational hazard.

Second Agers need to learn how to operate within the world of high risk. Not in terms of simply being "venture capitalists," putting up the money for someone else to take the risks, but "venture disciples," called to the greatest

> *Rock-and-roll? The most brutal, ugly, desperate, vicious form of expression it has been my misfortune to hear.*
>
> **FRANK SINATRA**

adventure the world has ever known: *following Jesus.* As the play-it-safe, risk-free, one-talent servant learned the hard way, the ultimate danger is not to risk anything. Anything good, especially rocking the world for God and the gospel, entails risk, innovation, and imagination.

Stuart Kauffman, the theoretical biologist and complexity scientist, talks about the "adjacent possible."[7] At any given moment, surrounding every person (and surrounding your church) there is a space of untapped potential, a halo of possibility and promise. Kauffman calls this his fourth general law of physics, the "adjacent possible." Change takes place when we risk redrawing our maps and rearranging in a new way our current configuration of things. It's not the one who takes the biggest steps who creates the biggest changes. Sometimes it's the smallest steps that create the biggest changes. The key is to step into the unknown, into the "adjacent possible."[8]

Second Agers are "movers and shakers" in training for Third Age world changing. Jesus "Never-will-I-leave-you / Never-will-I-forsake-you"[9] Christ is the ultimate "adjacent possible," the biggest expansion of possibilities in a world that needs rocking and real-ing.

14

CAT'S CRADLE

THE LAST PUBLIC APPEARANCE of singer-songwriter Harry Chapin was as commencement speaker at SUNY Geneseo on 16 May 1981. I sat next to him on the stage, as I had been selected by the student body to give the invocation and benediction for the ceremony. During the granting of diplomas, he and I talked under our breaths about the project he was finishing up, a musical he named *Cotton Patch Gospel*. About a month later, I received a handwritten letter in the mail from Harry, thanking me for the prayers I had offered and asking if I could send him a copy of one of them, since it had moved him deeply, even though he professed no faith.

Two months later, on 16 July 1981, thirty-eight-year-old Harry Chapin died in a car accident on the Long Island Expressway. I received a call from his wife, Sandy, who let me know that, as far as she knew, I was the last person her husband had written to. I then learned that she was the one who had written the classic song "Cat's in the Cradle" that Harry made famous—not just to commemorate the father-son relationship, but also to lament the way adults "grow out of" play and teach their children to value work over relationships, dotted lines over open tables, a "growing up" that Sandy Chapin testified her husband never did.[1]

———————————— ◇ ————————————

And the cat's in the cradle and the silver spoon

Little boy blue and the man on the moon

When you comin' home, Son, I don't know when,

But we'll get together then, Dad,

You know we'll have a good time then.

HARRY CHAPIN

Cat's cradle is also a children's game. It is played with string, in which various formations and designs are created by looping the string over your fingers and sharing the string with others. In order to create the cat's "cradle," you have to involve other pairs of hands. But as anyone who has ever played the game realizes, it is very hard to keep all the strings intact, and very easy to drop the strings or lose track of them. When that happens, your fingers become so entangled in the strands that you're almost immobilized and you must stop playing the game.

The key to cat's cradle is knowing which strands to pick up and which to let go.

The game of boxing has two powerful symbols, both conveyed by the same phrase: *Give it up*. When you "give it up" and "throw in the towel," you are saying in gestural form "I submit. I'm out." When you "give it up" and "throw your hat in the ring," you are saying in gestural form "I'm in. I'm entering the fray." For the Godplayer, a towel serves both purposes. To throw your hat in the ring is really to throw in the towel, because everything we do is done in a spirit of towel-and-basin service.

The key to the pleasures of the Second Age is knowing when "giving it up" is good and when "giving it up" is bad. Ever see the auditions on *American Idol*? Even after candidates have humiliated themselves in front of the judges, not to mention embarrassed themselves in front of the world, they come out saying, "This doesn't put a damper on my dreams. I'll never give up." When your dream is to sing, and you can't sing, it is of strategic importance to "give it up."

We need to let some things go, especially things that come not just with strings attached, but also shackles. Some things need to die in our lives: giving up a bad relationship that is dragging us downstream, giving up a bad career that is slaying our souls, giving up a bad grudge that is hanging on and hanging us up, giving up a dream when its pursuit causes untold health problems.[2] It is not for us to right all wrongs. Some crimes cannot be punished in this life. Some things must be left to go their own way. Some things bring with them insurmountable obstacles. Some ambitions won't stop shooting blanks or writing bad checks.

Among the strings on every person's lyre is a wire of warning that is apt to snap back or tremble with the rasp of a choice or direction that goes against the grain of the soul. But there is also a wire of love that tremors with passion at the pluck of a string that recognizes one's rightful place in the story. It is one thing to have "starting power" that can begin something new when the wire of love is plucked. But "starting power" needs "staying power," or what mountain culture calls "sticktoitivity" and the Bible calls *endurance*. What we know as *patience* in the Bible is better translated as *endurance*. And *endurance* is best defined as "impatient patience." It is easy to drop strings, to lose when splitting a log. Every blow of the ax is indispensable, but it is only the last blow that really counts. Persisting in one's effort to reach a goal often meets success. But a persistence that overrides the wire of warning is a Pyrrhic one.

At the end of our lives, each of us will need to decide when "giving up" means releasing ourselves to eternity, or unleashing within ourselves those healing energies that can put to death within us our former lives and allow us to accept our new lives. Either way, old life dies; new life is born.

Second Agers are not only pilgrim disciples who pick up others' stories along the way; they are also thread-safe storytellers with yarns that can be trusted and spun without "losing the thread" of the bigger story. The words *text* and *textile* are close relatives, because narratives are "woven" or "strung" out of strings and story lines. The word *line* itself comes from the Latin *linea*, a flaxen thread for making linen.[3] People talk about "drawing the line," "toeing the line," and "not stepping over the line." But the true *line* is Christ. Godplayers don't step over or beyond the story line of Christ. They make every line in the sand not a scrimmage line, but a Christ outline and Jesus story line.

In the Hebrew tradition, "string" is a very important metaphor for the covenant relationship. It is used extensively in the Hebrew Scriptures. The Torah uses the metaphor of a "garment" with the Word of Yahweh woven into the hem, and the *tzitzit*—four long threads, some white, some blue—attached at the four corners. These are called the

◇

A string that is always taut, breaks.

OLD PROVERB

"wings." These threads were thought to be the "healing power" of the garment (hence the refrain from the Wesley hymn, "risen with healing in his wings").[4]

People would long to touch the hem, or *tzitzit*, of the garments worn by rabbis and priests (including Jesus) in order to be healed. The metaphor "threads" is inherent also in the Hebrew language itself, in the genealogies of the covenant promise, and in other metaphors in the Jewish faith, such as the clothing of high priests, tapestries of the Tabernacle, and the idea behind the *tefillin* (the small leather boxes stuffed with Scripture verses and worn by observant Jewish men during their morning prayers). All these metaphors for the covenant relationship serve to remind the wearers that their hearts are bound to God.

In our Christian faith, the "ties that bind" our hearts in Christian love are embedded in the discipleship bond with Jesus the Messiah. The bond of Christ and the church, like the Hebrew bond between God and his people, are often compared to the marriage covenant. Relationships in the body of Christ are like the complex and beautiful patterns of the cat's cradle. They are born from the swaddle of the manger and unleashed by the unraveling of the cloths in the Resurrection and the tearing of the Temple veil in two.

The greatest "string" metaphor for Christians is the tie that binds all together in God's great worship playground known as the church. The church is not a community that works, but a community that plays and prays. The more Second Agers learn to play and pray, the more *real* connections they will make, and the more cat's cradle becomes healing play. As any therapist will tell you, all healing is play.

In the movie business, right after a film finishes shooting, there's a gathering called a *wrap party* (as in, "It's a wrap," meaning it's finished). The church needs more wrap parties to celebrate its variety of "missions accomplished" and healing play.

15

ANGRY BIRDS

ANGRY BIRDS, an app developed in Finland, has been downloaded more than five hundred million times across various platforms. It's a game played on mobile devices and is the current generation's equivalent of Pac-Man—except it has been much more successful. So successful, in fact, that the entire Finnish economy to some degree depends on the fate of the game's newest iteration, Angry Birds Star Wars. In terms of its social impact, Angry Birds has greater importance to the Finns than Nokia, a multinational technology company with headquarters near Helsinki.

Even without their own wrap party (Oscars, Grammys, Emmys), video game companies now generate more revenue than Hollywood and the music industry. As it pioneers new forms of digital creativity, the gaming industry serves as research and development for the wider culture, in the same way the space program became known as much for its ancillary products as for its rockets. The game developers have also created new forms of interactive research and

THE WELL-PLAYED LIFE

development. For example, Electronic Arts, publisher of The Sims, the most popular computer game ever sold, figures it owes 60 percent of its content to user-developers, who mostly gave their time for free.

Some people play Angry Birds. Others play "Angry God." Some people have the notion of an angry God. But Godplayers know that God is not angry at us. Julian of Norwich, the fourteenth-century mystic, wrote that if God were angry with us, even for a moment, we would cease to exist. Poet Edwin Muir deconverted from the strict Calvinism of his youth, partly because of his perceived portrayal of an angry God.

> *The word made flesh here is made word again,*
> *A word made word in flourish and arrogant crook.*
> *See there King Calvin with his iron pen,*
> *And God three angry letters in a book.* [1]

Some people play Angry Birds not on the screen, but in real life. "The miff tree" is an old metaphor that used to be passed along furtively from one pastor to another. Although other antique metaphors such as "up a creek without a paddle" are still in common use, "up the miff tree" is no longer in circulation, even though it inspired in its time many poems, songs, and even entire books.

> *Who has not heard of the Miff Tree!*
> *The most common thing under the sun!*
> *It grows without soil, like an air plant;*
> *And nearly everybody has one.*

It is easy to raise, it is started
    From a little slip of the tongue;
And almost before you know it,
    To giant proportions has grown.

It is handy to climb up into,
    When your feelings suffer a bump;
Or when the stock of your patience
    Meets with a sudden slump.

Its odor is not very inviting;
    But for that nobody cares.
For when you climb up in a Miff Tree,
    You always put on—airs.

Sometimes a great, thrifty Miff Tree,
    Will grow right in the church;
And though it looks rather peculiar,
    There's many a one on its perch.

If you would destroy a Miff Tree,
    Keep humility growing close by:
It drives all poison out of the air;
    And the tree will wither and die.

Or, if you would live in a place,
    Where the Miff Tree never does grow;
Just move into the Lord's dove-cote,
    Where his saints consort here below.[2]

Whether you recognize the metaphor or not, every person, not just every pastor, knows the miff tree. This skeletal, leafless plant makes roost for some gruesome birds whose feet have been trampled upon, whose feelings have been hurt, whose feathers have been ruffled. These are people who once "served" the church or were your friends until they flew up into the miff tree. Now they sit and stew, miffed and huffy, waiting like vultures for the first sign of weakness and blood. They also spew their wrath onto people below, dropping things on people's heads, just as the Birds pummel the Pigs in Angry Birds. One of the first things we learn in life is to treat people "up the miff tree" with long arms and kid gloves.

Unfortunately, followers of Jesus are often the Johnny Appleseeds of miff trees. Sometimes it seems as if Jesus wrote the handbook *How to Make Everyone, Everywhere, Mad at You.* The Good Shepherd leads his sheep into pastures that are green and good, not desolate and bad. But wolves will stalk, the wilderness will ambush, sheep will wander, other sheep will bleat. Some sheep you just can't please. Just read the book of Exodus, which is one big whine. You can't please some people, because they're never pleased with themselves.

◇

Hope has two beautiful daughters; their names are Anger and Courage. Anger at the way things are, and Courage to see that they do not remain the way they are.

AUGUSTINE

Truth is, we all fly into the miff tree. It's not just other people who are up there. We, too, are "angry birds"—elevating ourselves, sitting and stewing in spite and right, gathering in the branches with other miff birds, gossiping together about those "beneath" us, grooming each other in our grudge-holding, anger-nursing grievances.

The game Angry Birds has no point. Likewise, being an "angry bird" in the church is a pointless waste of time and spirit for everyone. "Angry Birds Miff Tree" is a useless, senseless "game" that harms us most of all and is the wrong form of "playing games" with God. We can't be in a loving relationship with God or others if we're up the miff tree.

An old railroad sign in the nineteenth century often puzzled passengers who saw it flash past their window. The sign read simply, "Shut Your Ashpan."[3]

"Shut Your Ashpan" warned engineers that the train was approaching a wooden bridge. The sign was posted at a sufficient distance to give them time to take necessary precautions to prevent live coals from the locomotive setting the bridge afire.

How many relationships have been ruptured, how many bridges burned, because we could not "shut our ashpans"? How often have we dropped some angry words or provoking phrase, some quick retorts or hasty speech, or spewed forth some hot coals from our smoking-hot lips and set old planks of friendship on fire?

"Angry birds" are highly combustible. But it isn't just anger that burns some bridges. In some "wooden bridge" occasions in life, words of almost any kind are sparks to tinder, and those who can recognize the danger signals and resist the urge to fling retorts in explanation or prevarication or vituperation will lower drawbridges instead of burning them.

In the Moroccan fable "The Birth of the Sahara," each grain of sand in the Great Desert represents a lie told by a human. The oases are traces of the garden that once covered the earth before the death of innocence.[4]

The best way to tame angry birds and turn them into songbirds is with prayer. Prayer is life's real play and recreation. The psalmist tells us what it means to please God with our prayers: "I give myself unto prayer."[5] Actually, this is best translated, "I am prayer." In a life of Godplay, all of life becomes a prayer, a "Lord's Prayer." As Origen puts it in his treatise on prayer, if we live in relationship with God, we are praying: "The entire life of the saint taken as a whole is a single great prayer."[6] Godplay is the creed and call of prayer.

◇

Speak when you are angry—and you will make the best speech you'll ever regret.

LAURENCE J. PETER

When I was living in Rochester, New York, I walked out to my car one drizzly day and found my neighbor watering his lawn.

"Why are you watering the lawn?" I asked playfully.

"Well, you know me," he replied. "I don't like to sit around."

As Henry David Thoreau said, "It is not enough to be industrious; so are the ants. What are you industrious about?"[7] Jesus invites us to join him in being about His Father's business (Luke 2:49).

Jesus didn't "find time" to pray amidst a bustling base of preaching, teaching, and healing; rather, his foundation of prayer sent him out to preach, teach, and heal. Unlike other religious traditions, which are muscle-bound in prayer practices and new strategies for praying (bells, wheels, whistles, and other prayer tools), Christianity has very little to say about *how* to pray. Jesus gave his disciples no method for prayer, as a guru would do, or some techniques for prayer, as a sage would do.

Jesus revolutionizes the practice of prayer, not by introducing new forms of prayer, but a new *focus* for praying. Prayer for Jesus is not about techniques, but trust. If we are to experience God as Jesus experiences God, which he instructed us to do, then Jesus' experience of God was not one of Absolute Other or Ground of Being or even as Creator of the Cosmos. Jesus experiences God as the loving Parent who has entered into this unique relationship with humankind and delights in our presence.[8]

Jesus invites us to experience God the same way, which shapes the practice of prayer into a very different form, one based on spontaneity and trust and intimacy, not structure and technique and wordy formality. No wonder the ideal pray-er for Jesus is a child.[9]

But he tells us what to pray for and in what spirit: Pray for the Kingdom, which will fulfill all our dreams and desires; and pray with an attitude of faith, of forgiveness, of bold endurance, and with one mind as one body.[10] This will bring people out of the miff tree and back into community, the essence of what it means to be a real player.

PART IV

Third Age (60–90+)
Master Player and Game Changer

16

NEWTON'S CRADLE

THE THIRD AGE is not when life winds down, but when life winds up. Third Agers must learn a theology of risk as much as Second Agers. The time until Jesus returns is not the time for rocking-chair readiness, indemnified dreams, or risk-free investments. The Third Age is the time to blaze new trails, find undiscovered truths, explore strange lands, search for better worlds in which to live and love. It is never too late in life to choose to be open to "the wounds of possibility."[1] To close down to those "wounds" is not to avoid risk, but it is to risk death rather than risk life.

Will you be built up, or brought low, by the touch of time? Your answer to that question may depend on whether or not you can play "Newton's Cradle."

Newton's Cradle, sometimes known as the executive's toy, finds its place on many an office desk. Based on Newtonian physics, the contraption usually consists of five to seven balls of equal weight, lined up in a row, attached by strings hanging from a frame. The physics behind the contraption is that when you raise and release the end ball on one of the sides, it will strike the others but come to rest. The ball or balls it strikes will not move either. The energy will flow through the other balls, which remain stationary, and the end ball on the other side will take flight in the same manner as the first ball that began the motion. The potential energy of the first ball, propelled by gravity, becomes kinetic energy when it strikes the next ball in line, passing the energy through each ball and into the one on the opposite end. What appears to be a simple row of balls is actually a demonstration of rather highbrow physics. What appears to be a paradox—one ball striking another, which oddly remains static—is actually a dynamic transference of energy.

⬦

The most beautiful thing we can experience is the mysterious. It is the source of all true art and all science. He to whom this emotion is a stranger, who can no longer pause to wonder and stand rapt in awe, is as good as dead: his eyes are closed.

ALBERT EINSTEIN

Such games are good examples of simple paradoxes. More sophisticated paradoxes might be those encountered in the thought experiment called Schrödinger's Cat, or in the interactions between particle physics and string theory. Ironically, it is science, almost more than any other arena of human inquiry, that has discovered *mystery*. Life is more paradox than law, more entanglement than elaboration, more enchantment than enlightenment, more multidimensional than unidirectional. In a world of information overload, where everyone makes daily petitions to "god Google," we are starting to burn out on knowing the answer to everything. Our mystery-mongering children will be nostalgic for the sensation of being clueless about some things.

Beyond our rational fixings of "what makes sense" lies a paradoxical flux of what cannot be nailed down. Take a plant. A leaf. A mollusk. A snowflake. Each is enormously complex. Yet each appears to us in sheer simplicity. Mathematics can create an elegant symmetrical fractal out of any material thing. Nature consists of what appears to be chaos, and yet chaos reveals an amazing beauty of perfect design.

The science called chaos theory is a science of this paradox. Life begins as a paradox: The moment you are born you begin to die. Discipleship is the journey of acquiring practice and accomplishment in the truth of paradox. In fully embracing the mystery of paradox, Third Agers become virtuosi in feats of simplicity and complexity: They sink deeply into faith, exude passion about the immense complexities of life, and welcome the unexpected winds of the Spirit. Mature disciples are master players of the game of life, and yet take on new challenges with joy and energy. Third Age disciples learn not to be so comfortable in habit, ritual, and tradition that they can't be comfort-able with change and randomness.

◇

I would like to paint a wooden spoon in such a way that people had an inkling of God!

KARIN BOYE, "A PAINTER'S WISH"

One of my daily practices in pursuit of a systemic—not systematic—theology, is what I call randomness rituals. My reading list consists of assorted volumes from diverse disciplines, many selected from the random recommendations of strangers and friends. I choose what to watch, not from a planned list or personal preferences, but from randomized probes. Creatologists have shown that the higher the randomness factor, the higher the creativity. The more brutal the conjunctions, the more oppositional the incoherence, the better to stimulate creativity. To force opposites together is to forge unimagined possibilities.

> She hadn't simply grown great, she had grown great simply.
>
> FANNIE HURST, SPEAKING OF SINGER MARIAN ANDERSON

The most creative Third Agers are masters of randomness. They relish the both/and juxtaposition of opposites. They delight in merging new ideas and in bridging oppositional relationships. Solid in their identity in Christ, Third Age Godplayers are not afraid to venture into unknown territories or to sail uncharted waters. They love new angles of vision and take paths not well marked. They are game changers, because they are not afraid to follow Jesus into places that seem odd or chaotic.

Jesus was a master juggler in paradoxes. The last shall be first. The margins become mainstream. A little child will lead chief scribes. Jesus destabilized the status quo by bringing opposites into relationship. This is why Nicholas of Cusa, the fifteenth-century philosopher, insisted that God is to be known only "beyond the coincidence of contradictories . . . and nowhere this side thereof."[2]

The essence of Godplay is playing with opposites, not so much a "coincidence" of opposites as a concatenation or dance of opposites. One might even make the case that the Christian faith is the most complex, and at the same time the simplest, of all religions. How about the Trinitarian notion of One God (radically simple monotheism) in Three Persons (astonishingly complex relationality)? The paradoxical "logic" of the Trinity may seem hard to wrap our heads around. But where fuzzy logic fails, simple faith flourishes. The theological edifice I am constructing in the course of my life is not a "systematic" theology, but a *systemic* and *aesthetic* theology built from the ground up and composed from the sound up. It is sound-made-sight—more a musical score than a textbook treatise.

The older I get, the more complex my theology becomes, but the more *simple* my faith is. Simplicity is a complex matter.

————— ◇ —————

There, the tongue wants to say and the brain too: the meaning of this is definitely that. Then the incandescent brass bell tolls: Never one thing. Never one thing.

ANDREW MOTION, "THE DEATH OF FRANCESCO BORROMINI"

Aging is a schizophrenic exercise in going opposite directions at the same time: I mature with age, and I immature with age. I call this *simplexity*. Simplexity is a systemic combination of both complexity and simplicity. The Holy Spirit reveals the God of simplexity.

The term *simplexity* derives from systems theory, where simplicity is complex, and complexity simple. The more complex a system becomes, the more simple its platform must be. In discipleship, the more the soul grows and grows up in the knowledge of God, the more simple our faith becomes. "But as many as received him," John's Gospel begins, "to them gave he power to become . . ."³ Faith is a "becoming." But a becoming of what? It is to become *children of God.* Children are the divas and "divos" of the divine.

Theology and faith coalesce in a dance. Just as we live in the world but are not of it, we need to understand the science of our world but be willing to live in an ecosystem of faith. Life is a play of paradox, more difficult to predict than the status of Schrödinger's Cat. Godplayers refuse to be martyrs to the predictable, whether social convention or ecclesiastical etiquette. Instead, Third Age Godplayers come alive to what they already know to be true while opening the lids and windows of the soul to the mysteries of The Door.⁴ I worry about people who know why bad things happen or think they can treat hurt with words and pain with clichés.

Wovon man nicht sprechen kann darüber muss man schweigen. [If you don't know what you're talking about, maybe you ought to keep your trap shut.]

LUDWIG WITTGENSTEIN

In a sense, Third Age disciples are chaos chasers, because to trust the Holy Spirit is to expect anything and plan nothing. The Holy Spirit is anything but predictable. If we follow the Spirit, we will have to be ready for anything, preparing for the unknown rather than planning for the known. The Inscrutable God invites us into an Unpredictable Life: "You . . . cannot tell where it comes from and where it goes. So is everyone who is born of the Spirit."⁵ Who can say where the miraculous might turn up, or where God is at play?

We have privileged our blueprints over God's finger-prints. We have lived our lives on Blackberry's calendar and Apple's tablet rather than heaving close to nature's bosom to coddle snowflakes in January, crocuses in February, daffodils in March, harebells in April, poppies in May, roses in June, cowslips in July, baby's breath in August, Queen Anne's lace in September, orchids in October, narcissus in November, and pansies in December. Because variety is the spice of life and God's mercies are "new every morning,"[6] Godplayers are the original spice girls and backstreet boys. Or as I tried once to put on a T-shirt, "Following Jesus Is One Hiccuppin' Hot Habanero Adventure."

We named our only daughter Soren, after Søren Kierkegaard, as a nomen omen. Kierkegaard described the "leap to faith" as a leap made *by* faith. In naming our daughter Soren, we prophesied her forward into the future, in hopes she would construct a faith in the course of her three ages like our ancestors built bridges over the great chasms. They flew a tiny kite over the chasm, which fell with its silken thread on the other side. The vast chasm was first leaped by a thread. But that thread was used to pull over a cord, and the cord a rope, and the rope a chain, and the chain a cable. And thus was built the bridge of steel, over whose steadfast span the massive trains thundered as they crisscrossed North America. The thread of faith, the "leap of faith," can become a rope and the rope a chain, and the chain a cable, and the cable a bridge, stretched out over the vast abyss of life.

In this "leap of faith" into the future, instead of trying to *prove* truth, we stand under something that can't be fully understood. In a sense, Godplayers don't know what they believe until they live their faith. Kierkegaard described Adam and Eve's "fall" as a leap into sin. That means to disensnare ourselves from sin, we must leap to faith. If, in our state of finiteness and fallenness, we take the leap to faith and gamble the mystery that goes beyond all understanding, we learn to gambol lamblike through life and play the game called Paradox. Our leap into the future need not be a headlong plunge, but it is not a risk-free jump.

This is not a surrender of reason in favor of faith, but a bringing together of the two in harmony. Confidence in the evidence of the known enables one to trust and play in the mystery of the unknown. If science alone is the path to truth, the results alone are an insult to the human mind and imagination.

Assurance is the ultimate mastery of simplexity. It is knowing Truth when we hear it and see it. It is loitering in the labyrinth of prayer. It is following the Way without having to count our steps. It is knowing that wherever we go, wherever we end up, God is already there. It is to have a core that never changes as it holds to Christ for dear life, and it is to have a circumference that never stays the same and even admits to some confusion. Or as one of my graduate students said to me, "Professor Sweet, I resent your

The LORD protects those of childlike faith; I was facing death, and he saved me.

PSALM 116:6, NLT

leaving me with the impression that if we knew as much as you did we'd be as confused as you are about some things."

Winston Churchill was right: "Out of intense complexities, intense simplicities emerge." For the past decade, I've been trying to forge faith's simplicities on the anvil of theology's complexities: "The Seven First Words of the Church,"[7] "The Whole Shebang in Six Words,"[8] "The Words You Most Want to Say to the One You Love,"[9] "The Bible in Five Lines and Seven Words."[10]

The Godplay life is one of simplicity of will ("Thy face, Lord, will I seek."); simplicity of desire ("Delight yourself in the Lord; and He will give you the desires of your heart."); simplicity of heart ("One thing remains: love."); simplicity of mind ("Set your minds on things above, not on earthly things."); simplicity of joy ("The joy of the Lord is your strength."); simplicity of devotion ("Worship the Lord your God and serve him only."); and simplicity of action ("Do all to the glory of God").[11] Part of the theological lumber in our edifice complex must be dedicated as scaffolding to lift up Christ. Or as Thomas Aquinas, whom some would call the greatest theologian in the history of the church, said about his magnum opus, the *Summa Theologica*, compared to Christ it is "nothing but straw, straw for burning."

We remember the Polish astronomer Nicolaus Copernicus for his scientific and mathematical genius. There is even a revolution named after him: the Copernican Revolution. But when he lay dying at Frauenberg, and his recently published magnum opus, *On the Revolutions of Heavenly Spheres*, was plopped in his lap, he didn't want to talk about astronomy.

He wanted to talk about Jesus and some lines by the poet-pope Aeneas Silvius (Pope Pius II) that would be inscribed on his monument at St. John's Church in his native city of Torun. Here is the inscription on the earliest monument to Copernicus:

I crave not the Grace bestowed on Paul
Nor the remission granted to Peter
Only forgive me, I fervently pray
As thou forgavest the crucified thieves.[12]

We all enter eternity the same way as did the convict convert on the cross, also known as the Penitent Thief: "Lord have mercy, Christ have mercy, Lord have mercy."

God said, "It is finished," and then rested from playing so hard. Jesus said, "It is finished," and then rested in the bosom of his Father. The Holy Spirit says in each one of us, "It is finished," a "Nunc Dimittis" of "Lord, now let thy servant depart in peace."

When the "Nunc Dimittis" time comes, every one of us will reckon life not by years but by months, then days, then hours. There comes a time in life when we cease planting both feet in this world and begin placing one foot into the next. When I take my last breaths, the words on my lips won't be snatches from my carefully constructed complex theological system. Nor will I be taking that great long sigh into the unknown for which Beethoven is known: "Must it be? It must be! It must be!"[13]

Rather, what will usher me into eternity is the simple faith of a simple heart that has "found a resting place, not in device or creed; I trust the ever-living One, his wounds for me they plead."[14] Life is a round trip. We all leave this world where

we started—as a child, carried home in the arms of a Parent after a long, exhausting day of play. The sadness of life is not of growing old, but of growing up. Be grown up in your theol-

I have always studied to be simple.

JOHN CALVIN

ogy, but never leave behind the faith of a child.

That's why I'll spend my last breaths humming or singing one or a combination of three songs: "Jesus Loves Me, This I Know," the "little ones'" lullaby that so captivated Karl Barth; "Children of the Heavenly Father," the Swedish lullaby written after Karolina Sandell-Berg watched in horror as her father fell overboard from a ship and drowned; or "Give Me Jesus," the slave spiritual that Ruth Bell Graham asked to have sung by Fernando Ortega at her funeral.[15]

And when I come to die,
Oh when I come to die,
And when I come to die,
Give me Jesus.
Give me Jesus,
Give me Jesus.

You may have all this world,
Give me Jesus.

If I am unable to rise in praise, I hope someone will sing to me the chorus of Canadian Steve Bell's blessing song "For the Journey," written in honor of his father:

> *May the Lord bless and keep you*
> *May His face shine upon you*
> *May His graciousness be like an endless stream*
> *May the Lord show His favor*
> *To your house and your neighbor*
> *Until last remaining strains of striving cease*
> *May He grant you peace.*[16]

Every doctrine I've been able to construct, every thought I've come up with, every wild idea I've dug up I will one day lay on the altar of eternity. And in the presence of Jesus, they will fade. Only the mystery and the paradox of eternal life will remain.

I'll love Thee in life, I will love Thee in death,
And praise Thee as long as Thou lendest me breath;
And say when the death-dew lies cold on my brow,
"If ever I loved Thee, my Jesus, 'tis now."

WILLIAM R. FEATHERSTON

17
TRUTH OR CONSEQUENCES

THIRD AGERS stop putting a price on everything and start having their own price: They can't be bought. A master player is a master sage who is on the right side of the divide between truth and falsehood.

In times past, sages and seers were semioticians, those who could read signs and see not only physically, but with a spiritual eye as well. The Hebrews called these elders *tzadikim*, much like the Native Americans called their village wise ones "medicine men" and "medicine women."

We are calling them Third Agers. They are master semioticians, who "understood the times and knew what [they] should do."[1] The age advant*age* enables Third Agers to see Jesus in people of all times, cultures, and places, and recognize Truth in its varied forms and faces. They read signs that point toward the resurrection of the world to a new life.

The game show *Truth or Consequences* started as an NBC radio program in 1940, led by Ralph Edwards. Current Second and Third Agers may remember it as a television show hosted by Bob Barker from 1956 to 1975. To play the game, a willing contestant had to answer a question correctly. Most of the questions were tricky, or quirky, or not easy to discern. If the "truth" could not be identified, there would be "consequences"—usually some kind of wacky stunt or surprise feat that the contestant was required to carry out.

> *Older people have the time, energy, and responsibility to do everything they can to help heal our broken world. And they don't have to worry about having an arrest record on their resumes.*
>
> BILL MCKIBBEN

The Bob Barker version of the show became known for its surprises at the end—often a surprise visit from the winner's long-lost relative or a return of a soldier from Vietnam or a reunion with forgotten family or friends. The reward for excelling in the game was not a material prize, but the joy of restored relationships. This made *Truth or Consequences* the most popular show on television, and Barker's signature good-bye a showcase of media history: "Hoping all your consequences are happy ones."

Truth or Consequences is Third Age play. All of life is a "game" of consequences. In a world where many people think of Jesus' Way, Truth, and Life as "unfollowable, unknowable, and unlivable,"[2] Third Agers reveal Jesus as followable, knowable, and livable, and they showcase the rewards for choosing the truth of the Christ-life: the joy of playing in God's presence and pleasure.

Like all good master players, Third Agers have picked up along the way various "tips" or "good gaming prompts" that help them keep their eyes on the Truth, their feet on the Way, and their hearts on the Life. In a sense, these "tips" are like candles that shed light on life's paths so that followers can recognize Jesus even (especially) in the darkest places. These "means of grace" reveal not only the Truth of Jesus in the world, but reveal the truth of our own limitations and neediness.

When we hear the name Victor Wooten, the first thing that comes to mind might be "musical icon," or even "world's greatest living bass player." But for those who have read the multitalented Wooten's novel, *The Music Lesson*, something else comes to mind. It's an exchange between Victor and Michael, his skateboarding, hoodie-wearing Native American music teacher. When Victor wanted to learn a Miles Davis piece, Michael started playing and invited Victor to join in.

You strove to reach it, you desired to achieve it, you were afraid you'd not reach it, and now, arriving, you complain. Everyone wishes to reach old age, but nobody wishes to be old.

ST. BERNARDINO OF SIENA

"What key are you in?"

"Play."

"What key?"

"Play!"

"Well tell me, then; when should I find the right notes?"

"You shouldn't."

"I shouldn't?"

"No! Not at first anyway. There is something more important you should find first."

"And what is that?"

"The *groove*! . . . Forget about your instrument. Forget about the key. Forget about technique. Hear and feel the groove. Then allow yourself to become part of Music."[3]

Like the little groove in the center of your upper lip, called the philtrum, or the grooved notch under your chin, or the groove in the middle of your tongue, "the Groove" is the merger line between the right and left sides of our bodies and brains. It is a sign of total integration of our whole being and a life lived in holistic integrity and trust.[4] Even people who think they aren't musical need to find the Groove, for each one of us is an artist of life. In his preface to *St. Mark's Rest,* a history of Venice, John Ruskin writes,

> Great nations write their autobiographies in three
> manuscripts—the book of their deeds, the book
> of their words, and the book of their art. Not one
> of these books can be understood unless we read
> the two others; but of the three, the only quite
> trustworthy one is the last.[5]

Not just great nations, but great churches, great communities, and great Third Agers.

Isaiah admonished the people of Israel to live in the Groove when he said, "Your integrity will go before you and the glory of the Lord behind you."[6] Our integrity is the pillar of fire by night and the pillar of cloud by day that points the way to freedom from the bondage of being other than who God made us to be—slaves of sin, addiction, ambition, money, opinions. Everyone dreams of escape, but following Jesus doesn't enable us to fulfill our fantasy life in some self-constructed Promised Land. He beckons us to enter more deeply into *whose* we are and *who* God made us to become.

Life in the Groove does not mean we are always right or possess the whole truth. Nobody has the whole truth, except God. Sometimes, God brings half-truths and partial truths together, even in conflict, to usher us into All Truth. Diversity is not to be celebrated as an end in itself—to do so trivializes the differences and minimizes the seriousness of the issues involved. But integrity accommodates those who differ and disagree, makes space for them, and does not quash them. There are only twelve notes on the chromatic scale—that's it. Yet the variety of sound and rhythm played from those twelve notes is staggering.

The Groove always tells the truth: not always the whole truth, not always nothing but the truth, but always the truth as opposed to merely what is true.

> *In everything which gives us the pure authentic feeling of beauty there is really the presence of God.*
> SIMONE WEIL

For example, it's "true" that a note, a trumpet, and a mosquito can all "fly" through the air. In a very thin sense of the word *fly*, that's true. But what's "true" is not "truth." It's a "true" that conceals the differences that make all the difference.

Paleontologist Stephen Jay Gould, who was a master essayist, wrote about his experience of a performance of Berlioz's "Requiem." Gould tried writing it down, he tried explaining it, he tried analyzing it from the standpoint of neuroscience, sociobiology, and musicology. He finally gave up, and concluded that his experience of music eluded his facility with language. All his scientific explanations and writing skills, while "true" in their own way, could never capture the "trues" and "truths" of the experience of music and life in the Groove.

Before his ascension, Jesus announced the ultimate Groove: "All power and authority has been given to Me in heaven and on earth."[7] In Sociology 101, we learn to distinguish between power and authority, but it's an advanced seminar we must take over and over again to learn how to keep the two in the Groove. In the exercise of his authority, Jesus did not display his power. In fact, he went to great lengths to muffle and hide the display of his power in the exercise of his authority. How many times did he say after a healing, "Tell no one"?[8] How many of the five thousand knew *how* they had been fed—"You feed them," Jesus had told his disciples—or only that they *were* fed? When authority can be exercised without showcasing power, that is the Jesus Groove, a groove that in the course of one's life will be tested, tried, and (if found true) by the Third Age will have transcended the Groove of Integrity to become something even greater: the Probity Groove.

◇

Power is not what we humanly think it is; power is the ability to sacrifice yourself for someone other than yourself.

DENNIS KINLAW

Third Agers can be musicians of God's love who have found the Groove and can teach us how life can be lived in the Groove. Or they can be miserable old sots. The older people get, the more they need allowance and permission to play and to be shown how to play—even instructions in how to play.

But if we are not to lose the Groove, for songs of love to keep singing, to beat back a senescent spirit, there must be daily practice. And nobody likes to "practice."

Jazz great Oscar Peterson was born in 1925 and grew up in Montreal. In the late 1950s, he moved to Toronto with his trio, and together with Phil Nimmons, another icon of Canadian jazz, they founded the Advanced School of Contemporary Music (ASCM) in an old house near the University of Toronto. The mission of ASCM was to give jazz musicians an opportunity to study in an academic setting, as well as a multiracial one: "A total of 51 students, including three Negroes, completed an intensive four-month course that included weekly private lessons, compulsory classroom instruction in both theory and piano, experimental group playing, and improvisation sessions."[9] Peterson's trio was one of the first integrated ensembles to play in the major world of jazz festivals.

————— ◇ —————

Music heard so deeply that it is not heard at all, but you are the music while the music lasts.

T. S. ELIOT

The philosophy that guided the school was one of impartation, not imitation. "We're not building robots," Peterson insisted. "First thing, we're not teaching a style. If you come into my classroom and play what I play, you're in trouble." Peterson implanted in each student the Five Ts for how to practice: touch, time, tone, technique, and taste. "If you want a career as a player, you're going to have to have a touch that's impeccable, your timing has to be beyond reproach, your tone exquisite, your technique flawless, and your taste a thing of beauty."[10]

Third Agers are in the best position to impart to others the Five Ts of a life of Truth lived in the Groove.

Under the weight of work, we loiter and lallygag our way through life. Undergirded by the airiness of play, we go lunging and laughing and luxuriating through life. If the lightness of touch is key to the Groove, the lightest of touches is a gift of the Third Age. Sometimes called an "aged agelessness," a lightness of being comes from one having seen and suffered much, but who manages to find wealth in life's losses as well as life's gains.

> *The symbol gives rise to the thought, but the thought always returns to and is informed by the symbol.*
>
> PAUL RICOEUR

Without Godplay, Christians suffer from a surfeit of seriousness. Part of the reason we are humorless is that we don't know our own stories well enough to play in them. Periodically, I post on one of my public Facebook walls a little humor from my pilot friend Daniel Lloyd, who loves to lighten up my day with puns and groaners. Here is one I posted during Lent of 2013: "If you think you are a little different, you are in good company. Moses was born a basket case."

I was totally unprepared for the blowback. Immediately, I became a glass case exhibit for "outright blasphemy." People began denouncing me for all sorts of slander, including "insulting the holy" and "profaning the sacred." One woman, after "sharing" my "shame" on her own Facebook wall, posted the following imperative: "Hit your knees hard, Leonard, and open the word of God."

The response was so severe it reminded me of a line from Harper Lee's *To Kill a Mockingbird*: "Sometimes the Bible in the hand of one man is worse than a whiskey bottle in the hand of [another]."[11] But then I realized that was precisely the problem: My downbeat attackers might have had the Bible in their hands, but they didn't have the story in their heads. They didn't know the story of the basket baby Moses in the bulrushes.

I keep forgetting that most Christians have been raised on the Bible as a register of verses and a record book of history, rather than as a repertoire of stories against which we measure ourselves and find ourselves being part of an unfolding universal drama. When I retold the original story, there was initially some defensive backpedaling. But soon stone silence. The stone-throwers slunk away, and the fury passed as quickly as it had come. To Christians without a sense of humor, I am tempted to say (with John McEnroe): "You cannot be serious!" And then I'd add, "And if you are serious, you can't be taken seriously." To pull off serious, we need play—the playful power of not taking ourselves too seriously. If true humor is laughing at ourselves, true humility is laughing *with others* at ourselves.

18

WALK THE GRID

IF THE GOLDEN-YEARS dream has been freedom from work, the dream of the Third Age is the freedom to play the field. But Third Age disciples redefine the golden years from repairing to a golf course community to repairing the world. Vibrant, active, engaged, and still too young to be old, "never before have so many people had so much experience and the time and capacity to do something significant with it," writes Marc Freedman, who coined the term *encore years* to describe this new life phase, in which we can look at Third Agers as silver-haired Mafia in rocking chairs, or as rock stars changing the world with their songs.[1]

Meaning in life is like happiness: We don't get it by pursuing it. We only experience meaning in life as it comes through things that don't aim at meaning, but at mission. I like to call the missional thrust of the Third Age "Gridwalking."

More than any other age, Third Agers understand how to play the field. Playing the field requires not just years of practice, but a missional attitude. Gridwalkers learn every corner of the mission field, just as good golfers walk the courses they play to get to know their field. Gridwalkers know their postal code. The world is their garden, their playing field.

In the movie *The Bone Collector*, Angelina Jolie plays a rookie cop named Amelia Donaghy, whose mentor is a disabled detective, Lincoln Rhyme, played by Denzel Washington. Training Amelia to look for clues by reading signs, Rhyme tells her to "walk the grid" to collect evidence.

"Pay attention holistically to your surroundings."

"I can't do this."

"You can do it. Yes you can. Yesterday you stopped a train. You can do anything you want when you put your mind to it."

"Don't work me, Rhyme. Just tell me what to do next."

"Very slowly, walk the grid. One foot in front of the other. I want you to look around you now. Remember, crime scenes are three-dimensional: floors, walls, and ceilings. . . . I'm going to walk you through collecting the evidence. You do everything exactly as I say."

Maureen Sharib, owner of a name-sourcing company called TechTrak.com, gives the same advice to her students: "Walk the grid."

> "Walking the grid" inside a target company means
> to "walk" through the front door of a company
> and freely investigate the environs in your mind.

◇

Old age is the climbing of a mountain. The higher you get, the more tired and breathless you become. But your view becomes much more extensive.

INGMAR BERGMAN

I always see the puzzled looks on the faces of my students when I say this in class. Not many people think to venture inside a company like this. Crime scenes are three-dimensional: floors, walls, and ceilings. So are sourcing jobs.[2]

People like Lincoln Rhyme and Maureen Sharib are acting as *semioticians*, interpreters looking for specific signs. Jesus also tells us to look for specific signs of our times. He calls us to exegete the images and metaphors of our culture, to pay attention to what God is doing in people's lives, and to deconstruct the scenarios in which we live, move, have our being, and engage with our mission.

Paul was a master Gridwalker. He immersed himself in the field, or grid, of the people to whom he was sent. He learned their language, plied their trades alongside them, studied their culture and their customs, and got a sense of their economic-political milieu. Paul approached people where they were, not where he wished they would be. Wherever Paul went, he walked the grid. He did not plop down the gospel story from on high, like a prefabricated box. He walked the grid until the gospel came to consciousness in the context of the culture.

The term "gospel grid" has been used to explain the process of establishing a framework for talking about the gospel. Although the gospel remains the same Good News, people need to view that truth within a framework they can understand. No one is better at playing with metaphors and reframing stories than Third Agers. This makes Third Age Gridwalkers masters at "minding God's business" in the world.

They are also master mentors, able to coach First and Second Agers in cultures of collaboration and innovation, and convey stories of what it's like to Great Walk and walk the grid. The best discipleship formation is one in which every disciple is coached and is a coach. The British have guides for "gridwalks," which are ways of being in a from-the-ground-up relationship with the countryside and all its features (Scottish lochs, South Coast beaches, mossy ruins, cottage gardens).

Likewise, followers of Jesus need "relationship coaches" to show us how to walk with God in everyday life. Third Agers know the field intimately and can serve as missional field guides for others to learn how to play the game of life in the culture in which they live.

In the world of crime scene investigation (CSI), on some of the most popular series on television today, there are certain mandates for walking the grid that can be useful to us as we learn to navigate the Third Age as Master Players and Game Changers.

Scene Recognition

One technique is called "scene recognition," which is the proper first scanning and securing of the grid itself.

The Third Age is far from resigning from active duty. Godplay calls for a re-signing of one's commission to be a world changer. And world changing starts with storytelling. Third Agers have the responsibility of re-signing old narratives and designing new narratives for the future.

There are no "standard operating procedures" anymore,

no recipes ("add eye of newt and toe of frog") or Swiss Army Knife methodologies. There are only narratives that create, deliver, and capture *resonance* (or value) for the Kingdom in ways that allow others to create, deliver, and capture resonance for the Kingdom as well. With strength and charm of voice, Third Agers tell the stories of Jesus in ways that synthesize all and resonate with all, give voice to the oppressed, ventriloquize those who are suffering, and build for the future.

In many ways, we need to flip the stereotypes of the generations. Instead of looking to youth for idealism and energy and the aged for the wisdom of experience, the wisdom of "experience" now belongs to youth, and the idealism and energy (and time to apply both) now belong to the new Third Agers. Any summing up should always be a summoning up.

There is the wisdom of how the world turns. Then there is the wisdom of how life turns: What makes a "good person" good? What makes a human humane? What makes a good life? What should be one's contribution to the world? In the modern world, where change was incremental at a generational rate, Third Agers held both wisdoms. In a Moore's law world, where change is exponential at a turnover rate of eighteen months, First Agers are now the repositories of the wisdom of experience, and Third Agers the repositories of the wisdom of how life turns.

———————— ◇ ————————

Speak unto the children of Israel,
that they go forward.

YAHWEH TO MOSES

Founts of wisdom along with the energy of playfulness, Third Agers help us re-sign our lives into a play mode with

God. They have rediscovered the secret of play. Master players, they help us find the Lord of the Garden even in the deserts of life.

Reframing the Grid

Once the grid has been scanned, it can be creatively reframed to release new insights and illuminations.

It's amazing what can be done with the right frame of mind. What is the right frame of mind for a Third Ager? To see oneself as a walker, not sitting in a rocker. However, far from the last third of one's life being merely a time of recreation, these years of maturity are a time of *re-creation*, the most creative and dynamic period of our lives. Third Age people can be the world's greatest impetus for positive change. The shoe of "world changer" fits the foot of play better than that of work.

In ancient cultures, one's way of walking revealed his or her social strata, politics, mind-set, feeling, ambitions, and connections. "A 'family gait' was no less distinctive than a 'family nose,'" one historian contends.[3] Jesus introduced his disciples to a new way of walking in the world. It was a pace not determined by parentage or personal status, but a stride that exhibits faith in God, hope for the future, and love toward all. It was a walk that disturbs familiar frames and assumptions.

Jonathan Edwards, USAmerica's greatest theologian, once admitted from pastoral experience, "It is much easier to get 'em to talk like saints than to act like saints."[4] No one does walk-the-talk better than Third Agers. They've done it all;

they've encountered all kinds of roadblocks. And still they walk. Full of faith, these seasoned disciples are the best people to show others how to walk and keep walking in the world, even when walking gets hard.

Brailling the Grid

Getting a fresh feel for the grid requires that we put on new walking shoes or even take off our shoes entirely. The Third Age is when we get a new grip on life.

It is time to banish the word *retirement*, or at least make it as enticing as gnawing on barbed wire. Third Agers don't retire. They may *re-tire*—that is, get some new treads—but in that re-treading they gain better traction for the real world where the rubber hits the road.

The Third Age is not a time to wind down, but to wind up and hit home runs. In an age where humans don't know how to be humane and in a world facing problems as intractable as collapsing economies, pandemics, climate change, species extinction, topsoil erosion, groundwater contamination, nuclear proliferation, mounting addictions, and the collapse of nation states, we need Jesus followers who can show how to retread humanity by putting that *e* at the end of *human*.

All journeys have a secret destination of which the traveler is unaware.

MARTIN BUBER

They also show us how to get up again and re-grip when we fall. They are steady and sturdy enough to keep others from falling. Good treads can help Third Agers adventure into places that are difficult and rugged; their grip on faith and life make them our most determined and undeterred disciples.

Searching the Grid: Inward Spiral Search

In an inward spiral search of the grid, we start at the perimeter and work toward the center using a spiral pattern. In every journey to unknown places, it's easy to become lost without some kind of rerouting or returning-to-the-center sensibility. To walk the grid entails an inward spiral search, a re-turning to one's first love.

Nobody worked harder than the church at Ephesus. They studied and followed Paul's teachings. They opposed false doctrine. They endured persecution and hardship.[5] They put most of our churches to shame in terms of sacrifice and good works. Yet Jesus said to these hardworking Christians: "I hold this against you: You have forsaken your first love. Remember the height from which you have fallen! Repent and do the things you did at first."[6] Jesus wants our love more than he wants our labors.

Walt Whitman once told of attending a lecture on astronomy. The hall became smoky, the air stale, and the professor's charts dull and unilluminating. "I could stand it no longer," Whitman admitted, "so I ran outdoors, threw my head up and communed with the stars firsthand." That's what Jesus wants us to do with him: commune with him firsthand. But instead we prefer to remain inside, to ransack charts and diagrams and lectures on religion, its doctrines, and its rituals.

British rabbi and broadcaster Lionel Blue once wrote an essay titled "An Extra Dinner Guest," in which he posed the question of whether we would get excited if God were truly present.

> We ask God in prayers to restore his presence to us—
> but most of us doubt whether his presence would
> be congenial company. If the Shekinah (the Divine
> Presence) sat next to us at table, would we enjoy
> our dinner more or less? Our instinctive reaction is
> immediately "less." The joy of God, the bliss, the
> warmth, the love, have been so poisoned by hidden
> guilt (most of it unjustified) and evasion (most
> justified) that we cannot worship God because we
> have given him the attributes of a "fiend," not friend.[7]

Many of us find pleasure in our *work* for God, our *occupation*, not in God's person and in the divine preoccupation of pleasuring and playing with us. We have rewritten the Westminster Shorter Catechism from "The chief *end* of man is to glorify God and enjoy him forever" to "The chief *means* of man is to glorify God and enjoy him forever toward occupational ends and lines of work."

Do we evangelize because Jesus can change someone's "wrongness" to "rightness"? Or do we evangelize because the pearl of great price, our experience of Christ, is so priceless we want others to experience "the riches of his grace"[8] and the sweetness of his presence?

Third Agers know how to find their way home to Christ

again and again. They have a built-in GPS that points them to Christ in every situation, and helps them remember their faith in the face of all that appears foreign, unknown, confusing, chaotic. A return is not just a *metanoia*, but a re-turn to origins, a re-turn to youth, a re-turn home, a re-turn to play, a re-turn to God.

Searching the Grid: Parallel Search
In a parallel grid search, all searchers form a line and walk it slowly. Sometimes there are two parallel searches going opposite ways: one vertical, one horizontal. It's most like a dance. *Vive la fête!* ("Long live the party!") Party on! Live it up! These are phrases we commonly use to describe the opposite of what it really means to "party on" and "live it up."

Lately it seems we have turned parties from celebrations into *causes*, from places where we meet for the sole purpose of enjoying other people into places where people gather to support a common concern, further aims, or fulfill some purpose—as potential consumers, future customers, improved contacts, possible sex partners.

The church used to give the best parties. Festivals were noisy, multisensory, sensual events with party planners who were the leading artists of their day: sets designed by Palladio, paintings by Rubens, music by Gabrieli. Partygoers dressed up in their most outlandish clothes, and the entire village became a stage for streets hung with fabrics, mock battles on the commons, games of horsemanship, and music and food everywhere, with public fountains flowing with wine.

Now it seems many Christians are allergic to parties, if

not outright opposed to them. I come from a tradition that was so opposed to any form of levity that it refused to condone even fund-raising that was fun. No bazaars, grab bags, fairs, festivals, carnivals, or anything that might appeal to "vanity or the love of pleasure." A party atmosphere "is contrary to the New Testament, and also a serious and weakening compromise on the church's part."[9]

In the church I grew up in, there was not only no partying, there was no bobbed hair and no pants for women, no shorts, no cussing, no makeup, no jewelry (at engagement, holiness women got a watch, not a ring), no feathers or flowers on one's clothes, no card playing, no movies, no dancing, no smoking, no drinking, no fiction (frivolity and fantasy were "wastes of time"). My teenage years were a minefield of "No!"s . . . and I detonated most of them.

The church has too often been a "No" place filled with "No" people. But to truly follow Jesus is to rattle off "Yes," not "No." A yes to Jesus, a yes to life, a yes to love, a yes to a lifelong party. Our first occupation in life is to glorify and give pleasure to God, not to "save souls." Life's first mission has not been replaced by "make disciples" or even "follow me." In the original world God created for Adam and Eve, there were no souls needing salvation, only God enjoying our worship and loving to play and party with us in the Garden.

Third Agers are the ultimate "Yes!" men and women. As the apostle Paul says, "Our message to you is not 'Yes' and 'No.' For the Son of God, Jesus Christ, . . . was not 'Yes' and 'No,' but in him it has always been 'Yes.'"[10]

Third Agers say *"Yes!"* to God, *yes* to play, *yes* to forgiveness, *yes* to challenge, *yes* to life.

————————————— ◇ —————————————

*I find the great thing in this world is not so much where we stand, as
in what direction we are moving. . . . We must sail sometimes with
the wind and sometimes against it, . . . but we must sail and not
drift nor lie at anchor.*

OLIVER WENDELL HOLMES SR.

Searching the Grid: Outward Spiral Search

When Jesus' life enters into our lives, we move from the inner
to the outer; we become real-izers of Christ. Master incarna-
tors real-ize Christ in the world, transforming master players
into game changers.

There is a fable in Marie Smith's collection of stories by
G. K. Chesterton, *Daylight and Nightmare*, in which a knight
conquers a dragon by taking refuge inside him.[11] This is how
Jesus saves the world: by taking up residence, not refuge,
inside us, where he continues to live his resurrection life and
"walk among" us.[12] Third Agers don't just imitate others;
they have learned to live a Christ life in all kinds of places
and to make Christ real for others.

When they walk the grid, they see the world with the
eyes of Christ, and incarnate Christ in order to real-ize a
different world. They are masters at the fresh retelling of the
stories of Jesus and other "twice-told tales" (à la Nathaniel

Hawthorne), through a seizing of the vujà dé (the opposite of déjà vu), which is the ability to look at something as if you had never seen it before, like viewing a well-known landscape through a distorting mirror, like viewing the world through the always fresh goggles of the gospel, not Google.[13]

Sketching and Studying the Grid

To sketch and study the grid is to analyze the evidence and reconstruct the story in collaboration with others. Third Agers walk the grid with others, mentoring them in finding the cues and clues of what God is up to in the world today so that they can join Jesus in what he's already doing. In automobile racing, drivers walk the grid before a race to advance their finesse and fitness for the conditions of the track. But what do we do when we can't get a sign or a sighting from the heavens? How do we know where to go when fog, clouds, blizzards, rain, hail, snow, whiteouts make all traditional means of navigation useless?

We re-mind ourselves through a process called *dead reckoning*. To "reckon" is to weigh something and consider it carefully. A "day of reckoning" is a time when history weighs in the balance. When my gramma said, "I reckon . . . ," what came next was a decision about something arrived at only in her time and on her terms—her head and heart had to come together. From then on, she was about as immovable from her "reckoning" as a mole from its hole. Dead reckoning is reached when the stories and practices become such a part of us that they are second nature, and we "trust our guts and gizzard," as my gramma used to describe "intuition."

Third Agers are also our best semiotic coaches, but we must not confuse re-minding with the yearning for nostalgia. We may no longer be worshiping a literal golden calf, but we worship lots of other golden objects. Each of us has a calf in Horeb. Each of us feeds a golden calf. Each of us manufactures gods who give us permission to do the things that the real God wouldn't. One of our biggest golden calves is a "golden age." I have always wanted to start an organization called the "National Association for the Advancement of Time," to end all nostalgia about the past.

> The light which experience gives is a lantern on the stern, which shines only on the waters behind us.
>
> SAMUEL TAYLOR COLERIDGE

Nostalgia is the dementia of the Third Age. You can't "wax nostalgic" about your childhood or adolescence when you're still a child or adolescent. Second Agers don't have time to be nostalgic. Nostalgia is a delusional desire for the "good old days," for a world that is no more, for some golden age that never existed but was built on a "make a wish" foundation. As Yiddish novelist Abraham Cahan puts it in his 1917 novel *The Rise of David Levinsky*, for some people "the gloomiest past is dearer than the brightest present."[14]

Jesus did not intend his church to be the world of yesterday full of yesterday's people. God is too imaginative to repeat yesterdays. The re-minding of the Third Age is both timely and timeless, the tincture of ethos on the canvas of the eternal—mobilized for the moment, addressed to the ages; in touch with the times, in tune with the Spirit.

Re-minding is the remembrance of play and time in the Garden. It is living the Garden life in the midst of every time and age. Third Agers show us how to rediscover our relationship with God in the midst of tragedy and to re-member commitments to God in the midst of temptation. Most of all, they remind us to play as children even in the midst of life's most ardent work culture.

Freedom to please God means being set free from seeking the honors, the perks, the privileges, and the applause that society confers on its "successful" ones, those who maintain best the social order and advance the status quo. Jesus is all about living by a higher order than any civil society or political economy.

We jump over some verses like mud puddles. "Beware when all speak well of you" may be the least quoted, most glossed over line in Scripture. Truth? Social success may be the greatest sign of a disciple's failure. Disciples of Jesus are ahead of their times, not in step with their times. Disciples of Jesus are society's outsiders, not insiders. Even when we're functioning within our culture, we do so as *outsiders*, not *insiders*. We take our cues from Christ, not custom or convention. We judge our success not by general consensus or social census, but by gospel intent.

19

PLAY BALL!

PEOPLE WHO DON'T KNOW Satchel Paige as one of the greatest pitchers of all time still know him as a source of wit and wisdom.

- "Don't look back. Something might be gaining on you."
- "How old would you be if you didn't know how old you are?"
- "Age is a case of mind over matter. If you don't mind, it don't matter."
- "I've said it once and I'll say it a hundred times: I'm forty-four years old."

After Paige had been forced to play almost his entire career in the Negro Leagues and minor leagues before Major League Baseball was integrated, Charlie Finley, owner of the Kansas City Athletics, brought the future Hall of Famer back for one game, in 1965. Then fifty-nine years old, Paige threw three scoreless innings against the Boston Red Sox before retiring for good. He remains the oldest player to appear in a major league baseball game.

Third Agers are the world's best and most misused resources. We put them out to pasture instead of letting them play the field. Given a chance to play, they can still play, and play hard. They are not just coaches, but frontline players as well. It's never too late to learn to play.

The Third Age is not about commemorating past pleasures, but finding pleasures in every day, on every page, through every person, to every last drop—whether plain-vanilla pleasures or double-Dutch-chocolate pleasures.

Third Agers have their own dragon stories to tell, spine-tingling tales of surviving multiple assaults of flesh-eating beliefs and soul-scorching choices. Third Agers inspire First and Second Agers with the joy and juice of drinking beauty, creating beauty, and bearing beauty. The Third Age glows *rubedo*, basking in God's pleasure, and sings *jubilato*, singing and shouting for the sheer joy of life. Enjoyment of life's gift and Giver, a life of transparence lived in the augmented reality of being "in" but not "of" the world, is what ultimately pleases God.

Third Age disciples have re-learned how to play. And they don't just play; they play hard. Having spent two-thirds of their lives playing, they now become masters at showing others how to play and how the game of life is well played out. They know when to pray and when to play, when to

---

◇

We need to learn to be old in a young way and young in an old way.

OLIVER O'DONOVAN

---

groove and when to move. They have nothing to prove and everything to improve. Third Agers find pleasure in nurturing younger disciples, struggling disciples, and the "little ones" of the faith. It is a time not just for reaping, but for sowing the best crops of their lives.

A recent study by the Kauffman Foundation found that USAmericans between the ages of fifty-five and sixty-four have launched more businesses than those between the ages of twenty and thirty-four in every year since 1966.

Henry Kissinger (born 1923) walks the corridors of government power, mingles with business tycoons, and dominates op-ed pages like almost no one else.

The average age of a Harley Davidson owner is fifty-two, and rising.

Benedictine monk Sebastian Moore (born 1917) is known more for his relatives than for his own scholarship. His nephew is Nicholas Lash, the great Cambridge church historian; his great-nephews are actors Ralph and Joseph Fiennes. Yet, Moore published what some say is his best book, *The Body of Christ: The Shudder of Blissful Truth*, in 2011.

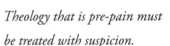

Theology that is pre-pain must be treated with suspicion.

WALTER BRUEGGEMANN

Chinese-American architect I. M. Pei (born 1917) designed the Rock and Roll Hall of Fame in 1995, at the age of seventy-eight.

British historian Gertrude Himmelfarb (born 1922) is still publishing blockbuster books and essays in her ninth decade.

Barbara Walters (born 1929) is one of the most powerful forces in broadcast journalism today.

The Beach Boys, who started recording in 1961, recorded a new album in 2011, and one new song debuted on the Top 10.

Think of some of our other dynamic voices from the past:

- Czeslaw Milosz wrote half of his poems after he was seventy.
- German mathematician Johannes Kepler gave the first proof of how logarithms worked in 1624 at the age of fifty-three.
- Golda Meir became prime minister of Israel at the age of seventy-one.
- At age sixty-three, Norwegian explorer and anthropologist Thor Heyerdahl navigated from the Persian Gulf to the Red Sea in a replica of an ancient Sumerian sailing craft.
- Author Willa Cather wrote her masterpiece *Death Comes for the Archbishop* at the age of fifty-four.
- Michelangelo single-handedly painted *The Last Judgment* on the ceiling of the Sistine Chapel at the age of fifty-nine.
- Horticulturalist Luther Burbank wrote his eight-volume *How Plants Are Trained to Work for Man* at the age of seventy-two.[1]

I love the story of the seventysomething woman with a mind of her own who returned home from the hospital after major surgery. Among other things, her doctor instructed her to take things easy for a while. Above all, she said, do not go up and down stairs until the next visit.

One week later, the doctor examined her, evaluated her incision and told her that she could safely go up and down the stairs again. To which the patient replied: "Thank God! I was getting tired climbing up and down that drainpipe!"

Why do we put our Third Agers out to pasture when we ought to be sending them out to pastor and preach and play?

From my own experience of seasoning, here is what I've noticed:

- My eyesight goes, but my insight grows. You tell me which is more important.
- My racquetball skills have plummeted, and some of my macho-muscle has become mucho mush. But I can plumb the depths of life more than ever. You tell me which is more important.
- I can't throw a football as far or a baseball as fast as my twenty-two-year-old son. But I can throw truth further, and pitch love faster than ever. You tell me which is more important.
- One of the biggest social assets of the Third Age is free time, or what Clay Shirky calls "cognitive surplus."[2] What if we were to harness this cognitive surplus of creativity, knowledge, and wisdom for global projects?
- In the First Age, we study in schools we did not build; in the Third Age, we build schools in which we will probably never study.

- In the First Age, we swim in pools we did not dig; in the Third Age, we dig pools in which we will probably never swim.
- In the First Age, we sit under branches and in the shade of trees we did not plant; in the Third Age, we plant trees under whose branches and shade we will probably never sit.
- In the First Age, we dance to music we did not write; in the Third Age, we write music to which we will probably never dance.
- In the First Age, we participate in a church we did not start; in the Third Age, we start churches in which we may not long participate.

If you want to make a dent in the world or "put a ding in the universe," as Steve Jobs said, get a Third Ager to do it. So often, we assign the most responsibility to those already carrying the heaviest loads of raising families, making a living, and struggling with life and faith. Churches have traditionally looked to Second Agers to mount up ministries and missions, and have overlooked the older "blue hairs," whom they have relegated as "retired from active ministry."

The years between fifty and seventy are the hardest. . . . You are always being asked to do things, and yet you are not decrepit enough to turn them down.

T. S. ELIOT

Godplayers understand that a pincer partnership of First Agers and Third Agers is our most powerful "natural resource" and our best hope for the future. But such cross-fertilization will not be easy. It is easy for young to love young, or for old to love young. But real love is the love of young for old and the love of old for old.

In the town of Gruyères, Switzerland, you can visit the caves where one of my favorite cheeses is aged: cave-aged Gruyère. Inside the cave, the guide says that, if we could see it, the air would be dense with little spores migrating from one wheel of cheese to another, each adding to another's complexity of flavor. Cross-fertilization is the essence of all creative periods, and the cross-fertilization of the First Age and Third Age can create something truly magnificent.

Listen to me . . . [you] whom I have carried since the womb, whom I have supported since you were conceived. Until your old age I shall be the same, until your hair is grey I shall carry you. As I have done, so I shall support you.

ISAIAH 46:3-4, NJB

Irish poet Patrick Kavanagh writes about two kinds of simplicity: the simplicity of *going away* (which I call the wisdom of the First Age), and the simplicity of *returning* (which I call the wisdom of the Third Age). The simplicity of returning "is the ultimate in sophistication," Kavanagh contends. "In the final simplicity we don't care whether we appear foolish or not. We talk of things that earlier would embarrass. We are satisfied with being ourselves, however small."[3]

Relationships built on the simplicity of return yield the biggest returns. I used to be afraid of people who were aged. But in my relationships with seniors, and my own growing seniority, I find that if you scratch a senior even a little bit, you find somebody's little girl or little boy. Inside every older person is a young person of a secret age—wondering what in the world happened. I tell my young seminary students to approach older parishioners with this in mind: Every one of them thinks they're your age. In their minds, they're exactly whatever age you are. I don't care if they're ninety years old; in their minds, they're whatever age you are.

We are all very simple at heart. When childhood is no longer at the heart of adulthood, the flowering of God's creative purpose withers and falls.

When our well-played lives are a sea of well-being, we don't need Ponce de León's fountain of youth or any magic potions to keep us young.

20

PLAY WITH FIRE

MANY, MANY YEARS AGO, a Colorado pioneer built a rock cabin. After the house was completed, he started a fire in the hearth. In a matter of seconds, the entire cabin became a burning holocaust. It seems the rocks were shale and were impregnated with oil. The oil had survived for centuries within the rock. But when the oil was touched by fire, it exploded instantly, releasing its untapped energy.

This is what happened at Pentecost in the book of Acts and what happens whenever we keep Pentecost. When God fires up our lives, God's Spirit fills us with the fiery power of heaven. The Holy Spirit does not give us anything special. The Spirit merely ignites dominant spiritual energies which have lain dormant all along.

Our lives are just like the oil shale rocks in that Colorado cabin. When God's Spirit is fanned into flame inside us, and Christ takes form within us, our souls explode with all kinds of spiritual possibilities. The Third Age can be when Jesus becomes so close to us, and his life so enters our lives, that it becomes hard to tell where his life begins and our lives end. As an old Russian saying puts it about two people who have grown old together—they are so close that when one cries the other tastes salt.

Third Agers are best poised to convert that potential energy, as in Newton's Cradle, into kinetic reality and set the world on fire. Ignited with the power of the Spirit, which empowers Christ in each one of us, they channel that energy to set heaven into motion on earth. Where the enticement of the First Age is to be *consumed* by passion and the enticement of the Second Age is to be *treadmilled* by passion, Third Agers are *fueled* by passion, sent out to light fires of challenge and change wherever they see tracks of Jesus in the world.

Episcopal priest David J. Schlafer, in his book *Playing with Fire*, uses the metaphors of play and fire to show how, for those "on fire" for Christ, "playing with fire" is "sacred."[1] Play becomes the baptismal DNA that runs deep in the shale of our bodies and souls and allows our clay to be pliable to the Master's touch. Just as the divine presence is depicted in the metaphor of the burning bush—on fire and yet not consumed—Third Age disciples can sizzle with love, burn with enthusiasm, and shine with the radiance of Christ's promises, having a flaming desire for life. Third Age disciples

> *We are the music-makers,*
> *And we are the dreamers of dreams . . .*
> *We are the movers and shakers*
> *Of the world for ever, it seems.*
> ARTHUR O'SHAUGHNESSY

make sparks fly in dark and dry places, while fueling others to be vehicles for God's mission in the world.

During World War II, scientific research became part of the USAmerican cultural identity. Parents wanted their children to grow up to be great scientists, like Jonas Salk, who might discover the next cure for disease or ignite the next breakthrough in industry. From innovations in vaccines and medicine to discoveries such as DNA and the new plastics, chemistry was hailed as the science that would catapult humanity forward.

When the scientific revolution was in full swing in the middle of the twentieth century, parents like mine, eager to "train" their kids in the basics of chemistry and to encourage *play* at science, saved their money to purchase chemistry sets, which were all the rage. My brothers and I were encouraged in the mixing of ingredients, the jumbling of formulas, and the triggering of chemical reactions. My father especially loved watching my brothers and me put down our Erector sets and open up our Handy Andy chemistry set to immerse ourselves in the world of science. I can still remember the feel of those beakers and the smell of the Bunsen burner as we played with chemicals to get them to fizz and explode. The Chemical Heritage Foundation in Philadelphia now houses the largest collection of chemistry sets from this period of the 1950s and 1960s, due to go on exhibit in 2014. The "practice" of chemistry

Jesus became wise, and he grew strong. God was pleased with him and so were the people.
LUKE 2:52, CEV

may have set a few kitchens on fire—our kit came with a small blowtorch—but the risks of "playing with fire" were considered par for the course if some budding Marie Curie or Thomas Edison suddenly discovered the cure for cancer.

Third Agers are best equipped to play with fire in following Jesus into difficult places. Daily practices of sanctification have become almost as obsolete in our lives as junior chemistry sets in today's bureaucracy-strangled, risk-management culture. Yet we cannot set the world on fire for God and the gospel if we are not "putting into play" our practices on a daily basis. Sanctification is the igniting of the spirit that combusts without consuming.

Just as infusing the contents of an aerosol pump into a bowl of soap bubbles will ignite if someone lights it, when we allow God to infuse the fire of the Holy Spirit deep into the inner recesses of our beings, we become combustible forces for truth, beauty, and goodness in the world.

◇

To be dead is to stop believing in the masterpieces we will begin tomorrow.

PATRICK KAVANAGH

The more we *practice* these sanctifying means of grace, these "sacred acts" of holiness, the more fired up we will be.

Dancing with the Holy One is the ultimate playing with fire. A dancing demeanor burns away doubt, disintegrates sin to ash, and changes one's life story. "Fire dances" are best done by Third Agers, who can testify to how the Lord of the Dance turns our Dance of Death ("*danse macabre*") into a Dance of Life with the Master Choreographer.

Oxford don John Wesley, the theological architect of Wesleyan Arminianism, wrote erudite notes on most of the Bible, as well as doctrinal treatises. But Wesley could not stop alluding to his faith as a "heart strangely warmed." Legal scholar and humanist John Calvin, the theological architect of Reformed Calvinism, wrote commentaries on most of the Bible, as well as doctrinal treatises. But his personal seal was that of a human hand holding a heart on fire. As theologically diverse as Wesleyan Arminianism and Reformed Calvinism are from each other, they are built on the same simple faith in God's redeeming power to set the heart ablaze, a common image that bridges and unites all theological differences and complexities. We can differ in the complexities but find unity in the singularity of a simple faith in Jesus Christ.

Third Agers make the best playmates and intimates of the Holy Spirit. Without gaudiness, gimmickry, or glibness, they can show us how life in the Spirit is not always flooded with sweetness and light, as in some "Christian" paintings, and they can teach us how to distinguish Holy Gosh from Holy Ghost.

Fire tenders are also story keepers. They make

───────────── ◇ ─────────────

For am I now seeking the favor of men, or of God? Or am I striving to please men? If I were still trying to please men, I would not be a bondservant of Christ.

GALATIANS 1:10, NASB

sure that the fire of the story keeps burning long after its passionate embers have cooled. But "playing with fire" for Third Agers is more than igniting a brandy flambé! Whether in purifying, healing, warming, or loving, Third Age disciples are energy conduits and change agents that glow with the fire of Pentecost.

Solomon's writings have typically been associated with the erotic verse of the Song of Songs and the wisdom literature of Ecclesiastes and Proverbs. While most scholars have argued that the eroticism of the Song must have been written when the king was young, and that, as he grew in maturity and stature, he penned the wisdom proverbs and precepts, recent thought challenges that view. Some Jewish scholars now believe that Solomon wrote his wisdom treatises in the earnestness of a serious and striving youth and wrote the Song of Songs when "relaxing into" the joy of love, life, and creation in his later years.[2]

Although we have no proof of which works Solomon wrote first or last, I like to believe it was the latter and that the Song of Songs is Solomon's realization that life is more poetry and play in the Sabbath Shalom of God, than a keeping of guidelines in order to abide in the world.

William Morris, the late-nineteenth-century English visionary and poet, writes, "Men fight and lose the battle, and the thing that they fought for comes about in spite of their defeat, and when it comes turns out not to be what they meant, and other men have to fight for what they meant under another name."[3]

At first these words seem depressingly pessimistic. But upon deeper reflection, they are realistic and grimly true. The long-term results of the battle each of us is called to fight are never in the hands of the immediate contenders. There are always forces and factors more powerful than we are. My capacity, and yours, for sin is limitless. Vanity and triviality are Goliaths that we fight every day.

But the human spirit, when under the control of God, is indomitable. What is required of us is obedience to the moment, our moment, every new moment, the moment God has given us, not the moment we would have chosen. If we take care of the obedience, God will take care of the outcomes. I did not bring my being into being. "I AM" precedes "I am." I am because "I AM" called me to be. My being is an obedience to and followership of God's being. The "being" with God is "fireplay."

Playing with fire is a reminder above all that out of death comes resurrection life. When we die, life is not departed; life is changed. From the ashes of humanness rise a "new creation" to inhabit the "mansions" in the eternity of God's *paradiso* and with our unique voice added to the annals of God's covenant. Each one of our "Third Testaments" is catalogued and open shelved in the library of the Kingdom.

A beautiful inscription was found on an old violin:

In arbore vivens, silebam, mortua cano

In the living tree I was silent, but when it died,
I began to sing

While living, I am like a silent tree, planted near running waters and bringing forth fruit. When I die, I will produce music like an old violin. My body will die, but my soul will live forever and sing the praises of God.

Conclusion

"YOU BRING ME GREAT PLEASURE!"

SOME PEOPLE FULFILL THEMSELVES. Some people are full of themselves. Some people are just full of it. Disciples of Jesus are full of Christ. But we are most fully Christ when we are at play. The surest sign of faith is the willingness to play.

In 1903, the city of Seattle hired the Olmsted Brothers firm to develop a master plan for a city park system. Rather than designing a centralized park, like Central Park in New York City, Seattle's decentralized plan located a park or playground within walking distance (one half mile) of every house.

The Well-Played Life envisions a similarly different "master plan": to turn every house, and every soul, into a park and playground, a park for God to play in, a playground for the abundant life of Godplay.

———— ◇ ————

Hang a tire swing on the tree of life and play.

KEVIN GLENN

All houses eventually fall into ruin and die, including this old house. One hopes, as Charles Wesley did his whole life, that the call and the course end together.[1] But our greatest hope is to hear God's original "It is good" spoken over each of our lives as it was at our baptism.

In fact, these words form the essence of the best and worst things any one of us can hear at the end of our lives. Either we will hear this music to our ears—"I've not just followed the comet trail of your life, searching for evidence that life was lived here. We've walked and talked together, you and me. We've had some struggles, some hard times. But we played the game of life together. It's been good. Well done. You've brought me great pleasure."

Or we will hear something else: "Depart from me. I take no pleasure in you."[2]

Don't "follow your bliss."[3] Follow God's pleasure.

We've had five hundred years of "making things work." Maybe it's time to start making things fun.

And never leave the playground.

Discussion Guide

This discussion guide is designed for a four-week group study of *The Well-Played Life*. Questions within each week are broken up by chapter so you can adjust for a shorter or longer study. Use this guide as a catalyst for developing a more "play-full" community, and for encouraging growth in your journey with Christ

Week 1: Read Introduction and Part I (chapters 1–5)

Introduction: Pleasing God Means Living in God's Pleasure

1. Leonard Sweet challenges us: "It's time to abolish work. It's time for a theology of play." What do you think he means by this? How would you define a "theology of play" for the Christian life?

2. Sweet says that sometimes we treat workaholism like a "glamorous plague." Why do you think we equate overwork with spiritual health and maturity? What is the antidote to this kind of thinking? Why do we often need "allowance" or "permission" to play in our lives?

3. The author asks some questions in the introduction that shouldn't just be rhetorical. How would you answer these questions: How do we make our lives as disciples a joyful, playful, and passionate experience of the gospel and not a drudgery of duty? What does it mean to please God in the nitty-gritty of life?

4. What does it mean to be a *personator* of Christ, rather than an *im*personator? What does personating Christ mean for the whole community as the body of Christ?

5. Sweet says, "The truth is, we've already been given everything we need to 'glorify God and enjoy Him forever.'" Remembering that pleasing God "is not a goal to be attained or an achievement to be sought," how do we make the shift from "Please, God?" to "Please God!"?

6. What does it mean to "walk with God" throughout your life? What would have to change in your life in order for you to become a more passionate Godplayer?

7. Leonard Sweet defines three Ages of life. Which Age are you in now? What are the essential questions that go with your current Age? How would you respond to those questions at this point in your life?

Chapter 1: The World Is My Garden

1. Sweet says that instead of fighting *for* victory, we should be fighting *from* or *on the basis of* victory." What do you think this means? How might your outlook on life change if you lived your life *from out of* your victory in Jesus?

2. Rather than a leading string, Sweet says the Holy Spirit is a "divine wire cutter" who breaks the cages the world puts us in. What cages has the Holy Spirit broken for you? What cages do you still hope the Spirit will cut open in your life?

3. "The Spirit does not stir our hearts to produce *works*, but to produce *faith*, *hope*, and *love* within us." Explain why you agree or disagree with this statement. How would changing your perspective from "works" to "faith, hope, and love" affect your day-to-day life, your attitude toward your job, your role in the church, the level of stress and worry in your life, and your choice of daily activities?

4. What does it mean to live your life as a *Shabbat Shalom* adventure? How would your life look different from the way you live it now?

Chapter 2: Follow the Leader

1. What do you think it means that the Holy Spirit of Christ lives *within* you? How is the "indwelling" of the Holy Spirit different from simply trying to act "like" Jesus? How does this distinction alter your commitment to Christ and your perception of God, yourself, and the world?

2. Instead of growing old, Sweet tells us we are called to grow *new*. How have you grown new over the course of your walk with God? What does it mean to grow new while your body grows old? In what areas of your life do you need Christ's help in growing "new"?

Chapter 3: Walk the Red Carpet

1. The author describes two ways in which we put ourselves at the center of the universe instead of following Jesus. We can be applause seekers, rebellious spirits, too proud to admit our dependence on God. Can you

name times in your life, or within your church, when praising Christ has been more about performance and perfection than surrender and joy? As a disciple, in what ways can you focus more on worshiping Christ with a humble heart?

2. To be Godplayers, we must first stand vulnerable and open before God—not as our photoshopped, politically correct selves, but as our real selves. In what ways do you hide from God? What discipleship practices can help you become more honest about yourself and more open to God's presence in your life?

3. What does it mean to live life as a "processional"? How can you move from "strutting your stuff" to "walking the pilgrim's walk"?

4. Leonard Sweet says, "The richness of human existence is grown not in the topsoil of our precociousness and 'strength,' but in the humus of our need and vulnerability." But most people do everything they can to conceal their weaknesses. How can we create a climate in which vulnerability is allowed, rewarded, and even celebrated?

Chapter 4: Cave Dwellers

1. Do you have a cave story? What about your cave experience most affected you? Did you find it frightening, exhilarating, or both?

2. In order to thrive, the author says that a plant—and a Christian—must grow downward and upward at the same time: down into the soil with roots, and up toward

the sky bearing fruit. What do you think it feels like to grow both directions in your life with Christ? What would your life look like to others if you were both firmly rooted and lavishly and creatively nourishing?

3. "True nobility of spirit is not just confessing our sins, but also retracing our steps and acknowledging our debts to our sources and sponsors." What "traditions and collective wisdom" of your ancestors do you need to "go back" to recover and rediscover?

Chapter 5: Partying in God's Adventure Story

1. Have you ever been told that God has a wonderful plan for your life? What do you think of Sweet's conclusion that God gives us a blue sky, not a blueprint? How would embracing that idea change your understanding of *life* and *direction*? How would it change your view of God?

2. Sweet writes, "One of the (many) criticisms of Jesus was that he enjoyed life a little too much." Is your life more "excessive celebration" or "sackcloth and ashes"? What would it mean to live each day of your life with a Christ-inspired party-like joy?

3. How can we re-create or rediscover a "celebratory culture," rather than a "celebrity culture," of Christianity?

4. "God's plan, simply stated, is this: *I've got you covered. I'll be there for you.*" How does this statement affect your understanding of what it means to *abide* in Christ? How does it affect your understanding of the Holy Spirit of Christ as *paraclete*, or our advocate to God?

Week 2: Read Part II (chapters 6–10)

Chapter 6: A Story Waiting to Happen

1. How would you answer the question "Who am I?" in terms of where you have been and where you are going? Why is it important not to ignore the past in forming our sense of identity? What is the danger in "starting from where you are"?

2. Leonard Sweet talks about how our identities are formed by the narratives, stories, and traditions that influenced us as children. What stories and traditions do you remember having an impact on you as a child? What Bible stories have helped to form your understanding of God and the world? How have those stories of Jesus shaped who you are today?

3. According to Sweet, the "images you open, the stories you choose" will determine your identity. What images and stories are you choosing to define your life? How have the stories and images you have chosen in the past affected your identity today?

4. If you are a First Ager following Jesus, how can you "re-member" yourself—that is, re-connect to who you are in God's eyes? If you are a Second or Third Ager, how can you help First Agers learn to "walk in the light"?

Chapter 7: Halo

1. Sweet calls the media messages we see every day "sermons." What cultural "sermons" do you see in the

world around you? What cultural "sermons" do you feel you have internalized?

2. How do you think Christians can *insulate*—but not isolate—themselves from the identity narratives that our culture propagates? How do you think a Christian combats those narratives in everyday life? How can your discipleship journey with Jesus strengthen you for your walk through the world?

3. In "The Tale of Iden T. Snatcher and the Storycatchers," what practical lessons do you learn about how to protect yourself in a media-saturated culture?

Chapter 8: Play in the Dirt

1. Leonard Sweet reminds us, "Holiness is the art of turning mud and dirt into vessels of beauty, goodness, and truth." What does this mean in terms of how you live your life for Jesus?

2. Why do you think we are so afraid of getting dirty in the act of living? What holds you back from getting down in the dirt in your life and out in the world? What do you think it means that "without hands made dirty in the clay, we can't learn, create, or interact with God's world"?

3. "To insulate (not isolate)" is to trust our Jesus Identity in a fallen world. What do you think it means to trust your Jesus Identity? Does this come easily to you, or is it a struggle? What would it look like for you to trust your Jesus Identity more than you do now?

Chapter 9: Ring around the Roses, We All Fall Down

1. "Failure is not in the falling. Failure is in not getting up again." Why do you think we feel so ashamed for falling? When you have fallen, how has Jesus helped you get back up again?

2. How does our Jesus Identity—our relationship with Jesus—help us recover from a fall?

3. Sweet emphasizes the importance of welcoming back our prodigals. Have you ever been a prodigal? Were you welcomed back? How do you think you, your small group, and your church can do a better job of welcoming and loving those who have fallen? How can we create rituals of restoration and redemption by which the fallen can be helped back to their feet and can resume being an accepted and loved part of our "body" of Christ?

Chapter 10: Cradle Song

1. How do music and song uniquely equip us to "trust in God . . . even in the most daunting conditions"?

2. Sweet says that a church that "sings together clings together." What do you think it means to "sing together"? How does singing with diverse voices in God's harmony bring about intimacy and unite the church?

3. Lullabies are sung not to put us to sleep, but to wake us up. Describe an experience when you felt as if you had been "awakened" to the presence of Christ in your life. What did that feel like? How did your life change after that moment?

Week 3: Read Part III (chapters 11–15)

Chapter 11: Dancing with the Stars

1. What does the author mean when he says, "The Second Age is a time of maturing, anointing, and commissioning"?

2. How are we in danger of "getting lost" in the Second Age? How can we prevent this?

3. Leonard Sweet says, "Self-worth is not best measured by standards of work or career, but by stories of enjoyment and pleasure" in your relationship with Christ. How do you tend to measure your self-worth? How can you begin to "take delight in life, not just in labor"?

4. Sweet says, "God is the ultimate synergizer." How can we better reflect God's image by making our work more like the creative act of play? How can we feel the joy of Christ's resurrection life, and the relational synergy we have from being in the yoke with Christ, permeate everything we do?

5. "Holiness is not about getting better at keeping God's commandments. Holiness is about getting better at enjoying God, paying attention to God . . . and reveling in God's pleasure." How did Jesus' definition of holiness differ from that of the Pharisees? How can we pay better attention to the love of God in our lives and in the lives of others? How can we become better at engaging intimately in relationship with God rather than trying to follow a rule book in order to earn God's favor?

Chapter 12: Rock, Paper, Scissors

1. Sweet says that, as Christians, we all translate the Jesus story into our own lives and become a "fifth Gospel," another personal story about Jesus' healing and saving power in our lives. How would you write your Gospel? What would the highlights of your fifth Gospel be?

2. We wear masks to hide ourselves from our selves, and ourselves from God. What masks do you wear? Do you wear them to hide your self from yourself, yourself from God, or both? What would it mean for your life and your relationships to make Christ the Rock your identity and to strip away those masks? How can Jesus help you to move toward a more "truth-full" life?

Chapter 13: Shake, Rattle, and Roll

1. "Second Agers are prone to get stuck on 'by the sweat of your brow you shall eat bread,' rather than 'my God shall supply all your need according to his riches in glory.'" In what ways have you gotten stuck? What can you do to begin having "a rattling good time" with God, trusting in God to bring you joy in the midst of difficulty and lift you out of every pitfall, to dance with you through life's peaks and valleys?

2. According to Sweet, "anything good in life puts *risk* into play." Have you ever hesitated to do something that Jesus called you to do, because of the risk involved? For followers of Jesus, how does *faith* play into *risk* in our lives?

3. A true sanctuary is a place where it is safe to take risks. Is your church, small group, or ministry a safe place for taking risks? What makes you feel that way? If not, what can you do to promote greater risk-taking?

Chapter 14: Cat's Cradle

1. One key distinction in the Christian life is knowing when giving up is right and when giving up is wrong. Can you think of a time in your life when you gave up, and it was either the right or wrong thing to do, in retrospect? What do you think determines whether giving something up is right or wrong?

2. What "strings" do you need to let go of in your life that are keeping you from "playing" in your relationship with God and others?

3. Sweet says that Christians are "thread-safe storytellers with yarns that can be trusted and spun without 'losing the thread' of the bigger story." Have you ever met anyone who embodied this always-awareness of the bigger picture? How can you keep track of the greater story in your many-threaded life?

4. What "strings" do you need to *add* to your life to bind yourself to God's story?

Chapter 15: Angry Birds

1. According to Leonard Sweet, we all sometimes get upset and fly up into the miff tree. What makes

you "miffed and huffy" with the world and with the church? How could you start coming down from that miff tree today?

2. Jesus wants us to pray with intimacy, spontaneity, and trust—like a child. How do you usually pray? How do you think you could cultivate a prayer life of intimacy, trust, and spontaneity?

3. What can you do to change your prayer life from something you "find time for" to something that is *foundational* for everything you do?

Week 4: Read Part IV (chapters 16–20) and Conclusion

Chapter 16: Newton's Cradle

1. "The Third Age is the time to blaze new trails, find undiscovered truths, explore strange lands, search for better worlds in which to live and love." How `does this description compare with your expectations or understanding of the Third Age in life? Do you find the author's vision invigorating or exhausting?

2. How has your journey prepared you to "fully embrace the mystery of paradox"? Give some examples of "simplexity" in your life and experience.

3. One way the author bolsters his theology is by reading random volumes from a number of disciplines. Do you have any "randomness rituals" in your life that enrich your understanding of God? What are some "randomness rituals" you would like to take up?

4. According to Sweet, to trust the Holy Spirit is to "expect anything and plan nothing." Do you agree with this statement? What do you think it would look like for you to trust the Holy Spirit and trust God's fingerprints more than your blueprints?

Chapter 17: Truth or Consequences

1. God doesn't want us to enter into some "self-constructed Promised Land," but rather to become more deeply who he wants us to be. If you could construct your Promised Land, what would it look like? How has Christ called you beyond that?

2. What does it mean to you to become "an artist of life" and live in "the Groove" with Christ? How does that differ from how you live now?

3. Sweet says that the reason we suffer from seriousness is that we don't know our stories well enough to play in them. Do you agree with this statement? What do you think it means to play in the stories we know of Jesus?

Chapter 18: Walk the Grid

1. Happiness and meaning do not come from the pursuit of either of those things, but rather from the pursuit of mission. In what ways have you experienced happiness and meaning while pursuing mission? How can you and your faith community focus on mission in this stage of your life?

2. How well do you "walk the grid," approaching people where they are rather than where you wish they would be? Describe how you might "establish a framework" with someone for talking about the gospel.

3. How can you serve as a "missional field guide" for First and Second Agers who need to learn how to play the game of life with Jesus within our culture?

4. How can Third Agers be world changers? How can you best bring idealism and energy into your relationships, instead of the dementia of nostalgia?

5. Sweet challenges us to love God more than we love our work *for* God, to be grounded in Jesus, not in fixing anyone's "rightness" or "wrongness." What would it mean for you to put *love* before *work* in all your relationships?

Chapter 19: Play Ball!

1. Third Agers have spine-tingling "dragon stories" to tell, and have experienced what it's like to walk with God through the mountains and valleys of life. What Third Agers have you met who have great stories? If you are a Third Ager, what "dragon stories" do you have and to whom would you like to tell them?

2. The cross-fertilization of First and Third Agers is essential to creativity and to fostering an embodied image of God. How have you cross-fertilized with people of different ages? What did you learn from

that experience? How can you do a better job of cross-fertilizing in your life and in your church body?

3. The Third Age "is a time not just for reaping, but for sowing the best crops of [our] lives." What seeds of faith are you sowing? With the time you have left in your life's journey, what can you do to "put a ding in the universe"? What can you do to nurture other disciples in their walks with Jesus?

Chapter 20: Play with Fire

1. Third Agers are *fueled* by passion, after the oil of the Holy Spirit has settled into their bones. What Third Agers have you seen who fit this description? What impact have they had on your life and your passion for Jesus?

2. "Third Agers are best equipped to play with fire in following Jesus into difficult places." As a Third Ager, what opportunities do you see for "putting into play" your wisdom, experience, and faith on a daily basis?

3. The practice of play is *necessary* to form us into combustible creatures of truth, beauty, and goodness. How do you think you can practice playing with God in your everyday life?

Conclusion: "You Bring Me Great Pleasure!"

1. Looking back on this book, what thoughts and ideas struck you the most? Was there any particular chapter, paragraph, or sentence that especially captured your attention? Why?

2. Sweet exhorts us *not* to "follow our bliss" and "make things work," but rather to follow God's pleasure and make things *fun*. Have these thoughts on play and work altered your view of God at all? How can you live your life for God's pleasure?

3. What does it mean to you to live a life that pleases God? Compose your own "life story" through words, music, or visual art to represent your personal vision for a God-pleasing life. (For an example, watch pilot Steve Scheibner's compelling video "In My Seat—A Pilot's Story from Sept. 10th-11th," available on YouTube.)

Scripture Versions

Notes

ACKNOWLEDGMENTS

1. Martin Luther, quoted in Mary Midgley, *Wisdom, Information, and Wonder: What Is Knowledge For?* (New York: Routledge, 1989), 252.
2. Anthony D. Pellegrini, ed., *The Future of Play Theory: A Multidisciplinary Inquiry into the Contributions of Brian Sutton-Smith* (State University of New York Press, 1995); Matthew Kaiser, *The World in Play: Portraits of a Victorian Concept* (Stanford University Press, 2011).

INTRODUCTION: PLEASING GOD MEANS LIVING IN GOD'S PLEASURE

1. You can find this story in Louis Albert Banks, *A Year's Prayer-Meeting Talks* (New York: Funk & Wagnalls, 1899), 204–205.
2. 1 Corinthians 3:21-22, NKJV
3. 1 Timothy 6:17, NKJV
4. Richard Walter, quoting Sigmund Freud, in Ben Wasserstein, "How *30 Rock* Made Office Life Fun," *Bloomberg Businessweek,* 17 January 2013.
5. Luther Ridgeway's "therapy of rocks and roses" included grinding rocks to make jewelry, especially for children, and growing roses to take to people who were sick and just to brighten people's lives.
6. Here is Alexandre Dumas: "In 1823 and 1824 it was the fashion to suffer from the lungs; everybody was consumptive, poets especially; it was good form to spit blood after each emotion that was at all sensational, and to die before reaching the age of thirty." Quoted in Clark Lawlor, *Consumption and Literature: The Making of the Romantic Disease* (New York: Palgrave Macmillan, 2007), 113.
7. "William Frank Harrington, 63, minister, dies," *Augusta Chronicle,* 4 March 1999, http://chronicle.augusta.com/stories/1999/03/04/met_255107.shtml.
8. Andy Martin, *The Boxer and the Goalkeeper: Sartre vs. Camus* (New York: Simon and Schuster, 2012).

9. 1 Peter 1:8, KJV
10. Psalm 118:17, KJB
11. Edna St. Vincent Millay, "Conscientious Objector."
12. Romans 12:11, MNT
13. Westminster Shorter Catechism, 1643.
14. Numbers 6:25, TLB
15. John 20:29, RSV
16. Psalm 96:9
17. 1 Thessalonians 4:1, MSG
18. Vincent Van Gogh, quoted in Laura Gascoigne, "Consoling Images," *The Tablet,* 30 January 2010, 26.
19. Ibid.
20. I owe the last half of this sentence to Facebook contributions from Colleen Butcher and Teri Hyrkas on 21 February 2013.
21. Colossians 2:15, NIV
22. This, in a nutshell, is the philosophy of Friedrich Schiller.
23. For Christianity as an "out-of-doors" spirituality, see my book *11 Genetic Gateways to a Spiritual Awakening* (Nashville: Abingdon, 1998).
24. Genesis 5:24, NIV
25. Jeremiah 12:1
26. Bishop Mathews, quoted in Anne Mathews-Younes, "The Life and Ministry of E. Stanley Jones" (PhD thesis, Wesley Theological Seminary, 2011), 24, footnote 27. http://www.scribd.com/doc/89277726/The-Life-and-Ministry-of-E-Stanley-Jones-by-Anne-Mathews-Younes.
27. G. K. Chesterton, *Orthodoxy* [1908] (Haddonfield, NJ: J. P. Piper, 2013), 77.
28. Simon Tugwell, *Ways of Imperfection: An Exploration of Christian Spirituality* (Springfield, IL: Templegate Publishers, 1985), 222.
29. See my 24 February 2013 contribution to *sermons.com* titled "Taking Up the Cross—Burden or Blessing?"
30. Matthew 11:28
31. Matthew 25:23, KJB
32. "Soldiers in the army of the upright" is Virginia Woolf's phrase. See Virginia Woolf, *On Being Ill* (Ashfield, MA: Paris Press, 2012), 12.
33. For more about the synchronicity of the *missional, relational,* and *incarnational,* see my book *So Beautiful: Divine Design for Life and the Church* (Colorado Springs, CO: David C. Cook, 2009).
34. Psalm 100:5, ISV
35. William Ian Miller, *Losing It* (New Haven, CT: Yale University Press, 2011), 7.

36. See my book *Viral: How Social Networking Is Poised to Ignite Revival* (Colorado Springs, CO: Waterbrook, 2012).

37. For more about the "ages of man," see Mary Dove, *The Perfect Age of Man's Life* (Cambridge: Cambridge University Press, 1986); J. A. Burrow, *The Ages of Man: A Study in Medieval Writing and Thought* (Oxford: Clarendon, 1986); Elizabeth Sears, *The Ages of Man: Medieval Interpretations of the Life Cycle* (Princeton, NJ: Princeton University Press, 1986). And, of course, there is always Shakespeare's "Seven Ages of Man" speech from *As You Like It* (Act II, Scene VII, lines 138–165) in which the seven ages of man are infant, schoolboy, lover, soldier, justice, pantaloon, and old man.

38. Peter Laslett, *A Fresh Map of Life: The Emergence of the Third Age* (London: Weidenfeld and Nicholson, 1989). See also Jacob S. Siegel's book review, "*A Fresh Map of Life: The Emergence of the Third Age*, by Peter Laslett" in *Population and Development Review* 16, no. 2 (1990): 363–367, http://www.jstor.org/discover/10.2307/1971596.

39. Cathy Severson, "Welcome to the Third Age," *RetireWow.com*, May 23, 2013, http://www.retirementlifematters.com/new-aging /welcome-to-the-third-age.

40. Charles Handy, *The Age of Unreason* (Boston: Harvard Business School Press, 1989), and *The Hungry Spirit* (New York: Broadway Books, 1998). The "four-age" theory was brought to America and implemented by Gail Sheehy in *New Passages* (New York: Random House, 1995). Peter Laslett and Charles Handy presented a paper together in 1991: "The Duties of the Third Age: Should They Form a National Trust for the Future?" *RSA Journal* 139, no. 5418 (May 1991): 386–392, http://www.jstor.org /discover/10.2307/41375550.

41. Interview with Carol Shields by Irene D'Souza, *herizons*, 2002, http:// www.herizons.ca/node/132.

42. For a different way of thinking about life in "three ages," see Irish management guru Charles Handy, *The Age of Unreason* (Boston: Harvard Business School Press, 1989).

43. Romans 11:29, NKJV

44. Elton John, quoted in Horace B. Deets, "Today's AARP: Public Policy Implications of an Aging Society," in *Biology of Aging: Disciplinary Approaches to Aging* (New York: Routledge, 2002), 140.

45. Norma Cohen, "Scientists Claim 72 Is the New 30," *Financial Times*, 26 February 2013, http://www.cnbc.com/id/100493887.

46. See Patricia Cohen, *In Our Prime: The Invention of Middle Age* (New York: Scribner, 2012). The category of "middle age" didn't even exist until

the mid-nineteenth century, when industrialists believed that a factory worker's most productive years ended at forty.

47. So argues anti-aging physician and bestselling author Ronald Klatz, who founded the American Academy of Anti-Aging Medicine (A4M). See also Verne Wheelwright, "Strategies for Living a Long Life," *The Futurist* 44, no. 6 (2010): 12. http://www.personalfutures.net/sitebuildercontent /sitebuilderfiles/StrategiesforLivingaLongLife.pdf.

48. "During the Cro-Magnon era, life expectancy was a meager eighteen years. By the time of the European Renaissance, a person could expect to see thirty birthdays, and by 1850 that number had risen to forty-three. Now, people born in Western societies can expect close to eighty birthdays." Sonia Arrison, *100 Plus: How the Coming Age of Longevity Will Change Everything, from Careers and Relationships to Family and Faith* (New York: Basic Books, 2011), 21.

49. Neal E. Cutler, *American Perceptions of Aging in the 21st Century* (Washington, DC: The National Council on the Aging, 2002): 6; http:// www.brown.edu/Courses/BI_278/projects/Aging/perceptions.pdf.

50. See the early twentieth-century hymn "O Young and Fearless Prophet" by S. Ralph Harlow: "O young and fearless Prophet / of ancient Galilee / Thy life is still a summons / to serve humanity / To make our thoughts and actions / less prone to please the crowd / To stand with humble courage / for truth with hearts uncowed; http://www.hymnsite.com /lyrics/umh444.sht.

51. I got this statistic from a review of Lewis Wolpert's book *You're Looking Very Well: The Surprising Nature of Getting Old*, in the *Times Literary Supplement*, 2 September 2011.

52. See my book *Nudge: Awakening Each Other to the God Who's Already There* (Colorado Springs, CO: David C. Cook, 2010).

53. For more on life's "witnesses," see my book *11 Indispensable Relationships You Can't Be Without*.

54. Ephesians 4:13, NRSV

55. 1 Corinthians 4:3-9, 19; 2 Corinthians 11:20-21

56. For the importance of the word *sprezzatura* to the life of faith, see my book *The Three Hardest Words in the World to Get Right* (Colorado Springs, CO: Waterbrook, 2006).

57. Avery Brooke, ed., *Celtic Prayers* (New York: Seabury Press, 1981), 48–51.

58. Mark 1:11

CHAPTER 1: THE WORLD IS MY GARDEN
1. Genesis 3:8-10
2. Ezekiel 34:11
3. The language of "seeker-sensitive worship" is all backward. Yes, there are

passages in the Bible, such as Isaiah 45:15 (NRSV), where God is hiding and we are seeking: "Truly, you are a God who hides himself, O God of Israel, the Savior." But God only veils the divine to preserve our free will and to shield us from being blinded by God's glory.

4. Luke 19:10, NIV
5. The notion of a Protestant work ethic was introduced and developed by Max Weber in his book *The Protestant Ethic and the Spirit of Capitalism* (London: Allen and Unwin, 1930).
6. "Where Did the Game Marco Polo Come From?" *Ask.com*, http://answers.ask.com/Society/History/where_did_the_game_marco_polo_come_from.
7. "Why was the game Marco Polo named after Marco Polo the explorer?" *Answers.com*, http://wiki.answers.com/Q/Why_was_the_game_Marco_Polo_named_after_Marco_Polo_the_explorer.
8. Abraham Heschel has written a masterpiece on the Sabbath simply titled *The Sabbath* (Farrar, Straus and Giroux, 1951).
9. Timothy Radcliffe, *Take the Plunge: Living Baptism and Confirmation* (London: Bloomsbury, 2012), 109.
10. The phrase "listening to the whisperings" is attributed to Steve Jobs in "Arianna Huffington on Burning Out at Work," *Bloomberg Businessweek*, 14 March 2013, http://www.businessweek.com/articles/2013-03-14/arianna-huffington-on-burning-out-at-work.
11. Abraham J. Karp, *The Jewish Way of Life and Thought* (New York: KTAV Publishing, 1981), 233.
12. Mary DeMuth, *Live Uncaged* (Rockwall, TX: Mary E. DeMuth, Inc., 2012), np.

CHAPTER 2: FOLLOW THE LEADER
1. Matthew 11:30, NKJV
2. Matthew 7:14
3. Barbara Jurgensen, *You're Out of Date, God?* (Grand Rapids, MI: Zondervan, 1971), 57–59.
4. Brooke, *Celtic Prayers*, 60–61.
5. Revelation 21:5, NKJV
6. Revelation 21:1, NKJV
7. Lamentations 3:22-23, NET
8. Robert Browning, "Rabbi Ben Ezra," in *Dramatis Personae* (1864).

CHAPTER 3: WALK THE RED CARPET
1. 2 Timothy 4:8, KJV
2. Colossians 3:3, NKJV
3. 1 Thessalonians 4:1, MSG

4. Jeremy Driscoll, *A Monk's Alphabet: Moments of Stillness in a Turning World* (Boston: New Seeds Books, 2006), 142.

5. For more on this, see my book *11 Indispensable Relationships You Can't Be Without.*

6. "Lord, I was born a ramblin' man" are lyrics made famous by the Allman Brothers Band, a group formed in 1969 and still touring.

7. John 4:14

8. Charles Taylor, *A Secular Age* (Cambridge, MA: Belknap Press, 2007).

9. 1 Peter 5:5

10. http://wesley.nnu.edu/john-wesley

11. Proverbs 31:25, NRSV

12. For more on the Song of Jesus, see Frank Viola's and my book *Jesus: A Theography* (Nashville: Thomas Nelson, 2012).

13. Acts 3:4-6, NRSV

CHAPTER 4: CAVE DWELLERS

1. Leonardo da Vinci, quoted in Timothy Ferris, *Coming of Age in the Milky Way* (New York: HarperCollins, 1988), 381.

2. Adullam: 1 Samuel 22:1-8; Engedi: 1 Samuel 23:29; 24:1-22; Makkedah: Joshua 10:16-21; Machpelah: Genesis 23:1-20; 50:13.

3. 1 Kings 19:1-18

4. John Pollock, *The Man Who Shook the World* (Wheaton, IL: Victor Books, 1972), 103.

5. G. K. Chesterton, quoted in Ronald Rolheiser, *The Holy Longing: The Search for a Christian Spirituality* (New York: Doubleday, 1999), 89–90.

6. Luke 4:38, 41; 5:12, 27; 7:2-3, 37-38; 8:27-28; 13:11-13; 14:2-4; 18:15-16, 35-42; 19:3-6

7. Luke 15:2, NIV

8. 1 Kings 19:11-18

9. Titus 2:12

10. 1 Corinthians 6:17

11. In *So Beautiful: Divine Design for Life and the Church* (Colorado Springs, CO: David C. Cook, 2009), I call this the MRI life—*missional, relational, incarnational.*

12. A gem of a book on these "landscapes" is Margaret Silf's *Landscapes of Prayer: Finding God in Your World and Your Life* (Oxford: Lion Hudson, 2011).

13. A powerful book on Mother Teresa's "dark night" is Paul Murray's *I Loved Jesus in the Night: Teresa of Calcutta—A Secret Revealed* (Brewster, MA: Paraclete Press, 2008).

14. See Genesis 1:28; 9:1, 7; 17:5-6; and 35:10-11.

NOTES

15. John 15:4-8, NASB
16. John 14:6; Matthew 28:19, NIV
17. Brennan Manning, *Abba's Child: The Cry of the Heart for Intimate Belonging* (Colorado Springs, CO: NavPress, 2002), 190.
18. To be "crowned with laurel" in our relationship with Jesus is to be clothed in his victory, power, and healing grace. To "bear the laurel" of the world's greatest lover is to be a visible sign, or evangelist, for his love.

CHAPTER 5: PARTYING IN GOD'S ADVENTURE STORY

1. David L. Larsen, *The Company of the Creative* (Grand Rapids, MI: Kregel, 1999), 250.
2. The story of the wedding in Cana is in John 2:1-10. For stories of missed parties, see the parable of the Prodigal Son (Luke 15:11-32), the story of the ten bridesmaids (Matthew 25:1-13), and Jesus' multiple feast or party stories (see Matthew 22:1-10; Luke 5:29; 14:1-23), some for people who didn't even know there was a party to begin with.
3. Luke 7:34, NIV
4. For Jesus as a glutton and wino, see Matthew 11:19.
5. George D. Watson, *Soul Food: Being Chapters on the Interior Life* (Cincinnati: M. W. Knapp, 1896), 135.
6. Katherine Duncan-Jones, "Time, Gentlemen, Please," *Times Literary Supplement*, 28 December 2012, 21–22.
7. Romans 12:10, RSV
8. This story is courtesy of Eric Baker and his daughter.
9. Proverbs 16:9, NASB
10. John 15:7-8, RSV

CHAPTER 6: A STORY WAITING TO HAPPEN

1. Peter Høeg, *Smilla's Sense of Snow* (New York: Farrar, Straus and Giroux, 1993).
2. Sally Lloyd-Jones, *The Jesus Storybook Bible: Every Story Whispers His Name* (Grand Rapids, MI: Zondervan, 2007), 17.
3. Proverbs 22:6
4. Genesis 16:8, NKJV
5. I am not even factoring into this discussion the phenomenon of Jews who became social scientists: Karl Marx, Èmile Durkheim, Georg Simmel, Raymond Aron, Hannah Arendt, Isaiah Berlin, Michael Walzer, Yosef Hayim Yerushalmi. The intense Jewish involvement in the social sciences—ranging from France's Marcel Mauss, Claude Lévi-Strauss, and Georges Friedmann through to Franz Boas, Edward Shils, David Riesman, and Daniel Bell in the United States—may stem partly from another source, as explained by Jürgen Habermas: "The Jews necessarily

269

had to experience society as something one collides with, and this became so persistent with them that they possessed, so to speak from birth, the sociological outlook." (Quoted in Pierre Birnbaum, *Geography of Hope: Exile, The Enlightenment, Disassimilation*, trans. the Board of Trustees of the Leland Stanford Junior University [Stanford: Stanford University Press, 2008, 4]).

6. I can't help but think here of David and Victoria ("Spice Girl") Beckham's invention of a christening ritual for their children, complete with an appearance by Elton John in a silver Rolls-Royce and a six-course meal rumored to cost £2,500 per head. David Beckham explained the occasion: "I definitely want Brooklyn to be christened, but I don't know into what religion yet." http://news.bbc.co.uk/2/hi/uk_news/4120477.stm.

7. For an excellent book on this theme, see David Dark, *The Sacredness of Questioning Everything* (Grand Rapids, MI: Zondervan, 2009).

8. For more on Jesus as the Question Man, not the Answer Man, see Christopher Bozung, *Uncommon Questions from an Extraordinary Savior* (Gonzalez, FL: Energion, 2012), and Conrad Gempf, *Jesus Asked* (Grand Rapids, MI: Zondervan, 2003).

9. See Thomas J. Meyers and Steven M. Nolt, *An Amish Patchwork: Indiana's Old Orders in the Modern World* (Bloomington, IN: Quarry Books, 2005), 13ff.

10. Even the name of Jesus can be a moniker of evil, as some Topeka Baptists have proven.

11. "If a way to the better there be," Thomas Hardy liked to say, "it lies in taking a full look at the worst." This was the basis of Ernest Becker's influential book *Escape from Evil* (New York: Free Press, 1975), which had such an impact on me. His thesis was that "man's natural and inevitable urge to deny mortality and achieve a heroic self-image are the root causes of human evil" (xvii). In other words, our very ingenuity, not our inhumanity, can be the source of our worst evils.

12. Philippians 4:8, NRSV

CHAPTER 7: HALO

1. Daniel Menaker, *A Good Talk: The Story and Skill of Conversation* (New York: Hachette, 2010), 125.

CHAPTER 8: PLAY IN THE DIRT

1. 1 Corinthians 3:9

2. Special thanks to my South African friend Tom Smith for his help in formulating this.

3. John Tyler Bonner, *Why Size Matters: From Bacteria to Blue Whales* (Princeton, NJ: Princeton University Press, 2006).

4. John 8:12, KJV
5. John 1:4-5

CHAPTER 9: RING AROUND THE ROSES, WE ALL FALL DOWN

1. Proverbs 24:16, RSV
2. Psalm 91:1, NKJV; Isaiah 49:2, NKJV

CHAPTER 10: CRADLE SONG

1. Luke 1:46-55, NIV
2. Luke 4:14-20, NIV
3. Psalm 22:26, NIV
4. Luke 1:46-55, NRSV
5. Matthew 6:2, WNT
6. Elizabeth Rooney, "Lullaby for a Christian."

CHAPTER 11: DANCING WITH THE STARS

1. See Pamela Slim, *Escape from Cubicle Nation: From Corporate Prisoner to Thriving Entrepreneur* (New York: Portfolio/Penguin, 2009).
2. The Starbucks franchise began when founder Howard Schultz read Ray Oldenberg's book about the importance of "third space" commons, *The Great Good Place*. I talk about this in my book *The Gospel According to Starbucks*.
3. Richard Tanner Pascale, *Managing on the Edge* (New York: Simon & Schuster, 1990), 64.
4. Charlotte Chandler, *The Ultimate Seduction* (New York: Doubleday, 1984), 3.
5. John Locke, *An Essay Concerning Human Understanding* (London: J. F. Dove, 1828), 549.
6. The Peter Principle was named after management professor Laurence J. Peter, who first formulated it in 1969. See Laurence J. Peter and Raymond Hull, *The Peter Principle: Why Things Always Go Wrong* (New York: HarperCollins, 2009).
7. Daniel H. Pink, *Free Agent Nation: The Future of Working for Yourself* (New York: Warner, 2001), 78.
8. Romans 8:28, NKJV
9. Mark 16:20, RSV
10. For more on Aquinas and *prudentia*, see Timothy Radcliffe, *Why Go to Church?: The Drama of the Eucharist* (New York: Continuum, 2008), 181.
11. For more on this distinction, see David G. Benner, *Soulful Spirituality: Becoming Fully Alive and Deeply Human* (Grand Rapids, MI: Brazos, 2011), 75.

12. Robert Frost, "Two Tramps in Mud Time" (1934).

13. Isaiah 55:2, NASB

14. "Hardening of the categories" was first identified by Joel Arthur Barker in his book *Paradigms: The Business of Discovering the Future* (New York: HarperCollins, 1992), 155, and often results in what he calls "paradigm paralysis." "Hardening of the oughteries" is Frank Lake's classic description of a common spiritual condition. See his *Clinical Theology: A Theological and Psychological Basis to Clinical Pastoral Care*, vol. 1 (Lexington, KY: Emeth, 2005), back cover.

15. R. P. Blackmur, "A Critic's Job of Work," in *Selected Essays of R. P. Blackmur*, Denis Donoghue, ed. (New York: Ecco Press, 1986), 19.

16. Psalm 1:1

17. Thanks to Dan Johnson for first helping me formulate this analogy.

18. 2 Corinthians 5:14, KJB

19. James 2:26, NKJV

20. A friend of mine, Michael Todd, recently made this comment on my Facebook page when I shared Luther's quote.

21. Fanny J. Crosby, "Blessed Assurance" (1873).

22. With reference to Psalm 48:13-14, see *Midrash Shir ha-Shirim* 7:1.

23. See 1 Samuel 19:24.

24. 2 Samuel 6:14-15

25. *Chariots of Fire* is a 1981 film about two British athletes at the 1924 Olympics. In the film, runner Eric Liddell says, "I believe God made me for a purpose, but he also made me fast. And when I run I feel His pleasure"; http://www.imdb.com/title/tt0082158/trivia?tab=qt&ref_=tt_trv_qu.

26. John Stuart Mill argued long ago that happiness did not come from pursuing it, but was a by-product of pursuing some other goal: "If otherwise fortunately circumstanced you will inhale happiness with the air you breathe." John Stuart Mill, *Autobiography* [1873] (London: Penguin, 1989), 118.

27. 1 Corinthians 13:4-8; 1 John 4:8

28. See my book *Learn to Dance the SoulSalsa: 17 Surprising Steps for Godly Living in the 21st Century* (Grand Rapids, MI: Zondervan, 2000).

29. Quoted in the *Times Literary Supplement*, 15 June 2012, 9.

30. Mihaly Csikszentmihalyi, *Flow: The Psychology of Optimal Experience* (New York: HarperPerennial, 1990), 47.

CHAPTER 12: ROCK, PAPER, SCISSORS

1. For more on "nudge" evangelism, see my book *Nudge: Awakening Each Other to the God Who's Already There* (Colorado Springs, CO: David C. Cook, 2010).
2. See Jeremiah 31:33.
3. See Ephesians 2:19-22.
4. Sydney Carter, "Lord of the Dance" (1963).

CHAPTER 13: SHAKE, RATTLE, AND ROLL

1. Matthew 10:14, NKJV
2. Genesis 3:19; Philippians 4:19, KJV
3. See Amotz and Avishag Zahavi, *The Handicap Principle: A Missing Piece of Darwin's Puzzle* (Oxford University Press, 1997).
4. Revelation 3:16, RSV
5. This is a refrain from the 1887 gospel song "Leaning on the Everlasting Arms" by Anthony Showalter and Elisha Hoffman, which was the theme song for the 2010 remake of *True Grit*.
6. Exodus 14:15, ESV
7. Stuart Kauffman, "Breaking the Galilean Spell: An Open Universe," *13.7: Cosmos and Culture*, NPR, 30 December 2009, http://www.npr.org /blogs/13.7/2009/12/breaking_the_galilean_spell_an.html. See also Ursula Goodenough, "Emergence into the Adjacent Possible," *13.7: Cosmos and Culture*, NPR, 2 January 2010, http://www.npr.org /blogs/13.7/2010/01/emergence_into_the_adjacent_po_2.html.
8. Saul Kaplan, *The Business Model Innovation Factory: How to Stay Relevant When the World Is Changing* (Hoboken, NJ: John Wiley and Sons, 2012), 119–121.
9. Hebrews 13:5, NIV

CHAPTER 14: CAT'S CRADLE

1. Mike Grayeb, "Behind the Song: Cat's in the Cradle," *Circle!*, Winter 2004, http://harrychapin.com/circle/winter04/behind.htm.
2. Psychologists Gregory Miller and Carsten Wrosch studied teenagers over the course of a year, using an instrument they developed to distinguish between people who either persist or let go when faced with a difficult goal. They found that the less tenacious teens had lower levels of the protein CRP, an indicator of bodily inflammation. Because inflammation has been linked with serious diseases such as diabetes and heart disease, the psychologists suggest that it may be advantageous to cut one's losses in the face of insurmountable obstacles. See Gregory E. Miller and Carsten Wrosch, "You've Gotta Know When to Fold 'Em:

Goal Disengagement and Systemic Inflammation in Adolescence," *Psychological Science*, vol. 18, no. 9 (September 2007): 773–777.

3. Margaret Visser, *The Geometry of Love* (New York: North Point Press, 2000), 31.

4. "But to you who honor and respect my Name shall the Sun of Righteousness arise with healing in His wings [*tzitzit*]" (Malachi 4:2).

CHAPTER 15: ANGRY BIRDS

1. Edwin Muir, "The Incarnate One," *Collected Poems* (London: Faber and Faber, 1960), 228.

2. "The Miff Tree," *The Standard*, vol. 56, no. 28, 13 March 1909, 18 (850).

3. "Shut Your Ashpan," *Watertown Gazette*, 12 March 1909.

4. This story is found in Richard Hamilton, *The Last Storytellers: Tales from the Heart of Morocco* (London: I. B. Tauris, 2011), 61–62.

5. Psalm 109:4, KJV

6. Origen, *Origen: An Exhortation to Martyrdom, Prayer, and Selected Works*, Rowan A. Greer, trans. (Mahwah, NJ: Paulist Press, 1979), 104.

7. Henry David Thoreau, in a letter to his friend H. G. O. Blake, 16 November 1857.

8. We have the text of three of Jesus' prayers. First, the outburst of thanksgiving at the return of his disciples from their first mission (Luke 10:21ff; Matthew 11:25-30). Second, the agonized cry at Gethsemane (Mark 14:36; Luke 22:42; Matthew 26:39). Third, the victory song from the cross, his singing recital of Psalm 22 (Mark 15:34; Matthew 27:46).

9. Mark 10:15; Luke 18:17. For Jesus' denunciation of showy spiritualities, see Matthew 6:5ff.

10. Luke 11:2; Mark 11:24; Matthew 21:22; Mark 11:25; Luke 18:1-8; Matthew 18:19ff.

CHAPTER 16: NEWTON'S CRADLE

1. The "wounds of possibility" is a phrase widely attributed to Søren Kierkegaard.

2. Nicholas of Cusa (1453), *The Vision of God* (New York: Cosimo, 2007), 45.

3. John 1:12, KJV

4. John 10:7

5. John 3:8, NKJV

6. Lamentations 3:23, KJV

7. Anxious-Nothing/Prayer-Everything/Thankful-Anything/PEACE.

8. Come Down–Come Out–Come Home.

9. "Thank you . . . Help me . . . I love you . . . I'm sorry . . . Be with me." See Marian Cowan and John Carroll Futrell, *The Spiritual Exercises of St.*

Ignatius of Loyola: A Handbook for Directors (Shelton, CT: Le Jacq, 1981): The Ignatian tradition is to say these words to God. See something similar in Anne Lamott's *Help, Thanks, Wow: The Three Essential Prayers* (New York: Riverhead, 2012).

10. God lead you, / God feed you, / God seed you, / God weed you, / God speed you.

11. Psalm 27:8, KJV; Psalm 37:4, NASB; 1 Corinthians 13:13; Colossians 3:2, NIV; Nehemiah 8:10, NIV; Luke 4:8, NIV; 1 Corinthians 10:31, NKJV

12. See Arthur Koestler, *The Sleepwalkers: A History of Man's Changing Vision of the Universe* (New York: Arkana/Penguin, 1989), 190. A later, more famous seventeenth-century inscription by Christian Wermuth is in Gotha, Germany.

13. From the final movement of Beethoven's Op. 135 quartet, "Der schwer gefasste Entschluss" ("The difficult resolution").

14. Lidie H. Edmunds (Eliza E. Hewitt), "My Faith Has Found a Resting Place," *Songs of Joy and Gladness, No. 2* (McDonald and Gill, 1891).

15. You can see Fernando Ortega's tribute on YouTube: http://www.youtube .com/watch?v=vu2E2FUcIiE.

16. Steve Bell, "For the Journey," http://stevebell .com/2007/06/for-the-journey-2.

CHAPTER 17: TRUTH OR CONSEQUENCES

1. Spoken of the tribe of Issachar in 1 Chronicles 12:32, NIV.

2. A. N. Wilson, *How Can We Know?* (New York: Atheneum, 1985), x.

3. Excerpted from Victor L. Wooten, *The Music Lesson: A Spiritual Search for Growth Through Music* (New York: Berkley Books, 2006), 28–31.

4. See Gabriel Josipovici, *On Trust: Art and the Temptations of Suspicion* (Yale University Press, 1999). Some have called *On Trust* "the finest critical monograph of the 1990s."

5. *The Works of John Ruskin*, Cambridge Library Collection, vol. 24 (New York: Cambridge University Press, 2009), 203.

6. Isaiah 58:8

7. Matthew 28:18

8. See Matthew 8:4; Matthew 9:30; Mark 1:43-44; Mark 5:43; Mark 7:36.

9. "Oscar Peterson's Jazz School," copyright © Johnson Publishing Company, Inc. All rights reserved; http://f.cl.ly /items/2b1B270T1v1V2Y2j0Q0x/Oscar%20Peterson's%20Jazz%20 School.pdf. Notice the advertisements (especially the Harlemite shirt and Kentucky bourbon). Thanks to Colleen Butcher for finding this resource.

10. See Gene Lees, *Oscar Peterson: The Will to Swing* (New York: Cooper

Square Press, 2000) for one of the better biographies of Peterson, full of detailed stories of his life.

11. Harper Lee, *To Kill a Mockingbird* (New York: Grand Central, 1960), 60.

CHAPTER 18: WALK THE GRID

1. Marc Freedman, *Encore: Finding Work That Matters in the Second Half of Life* (New York: Public Affairs, 2007).

2. Maureen Sharib, "Walk the Grid," ere.net, http://www.ere.net/2008/08/27/walk-the-grid.

3. Timothy M. O'Sullivan, *Walking in Roman Culture* (Cambridge: Cambridge University Press, 2011), 16. In this little book, the product of years of research, the author explores the relationship in the ancient Roman world between gait and identity. O'Sullivan also observed the marriage of walk and talk in Roman culture—talking was attached to walking, and vice versa.

4. Laurence L. Edwards quoting Jonathan Edwards in *CrossCurrents*, summer 1995, 257.

5. Acts 20:28-31; Revelation 2:2

6. Revelation 2:4-5, NIV

7. Lionel Blue, *Day Trips to Eternity* (London: Darton, Longman & Todd, 1987), 16.

8. Ephesians 1:7, KJV

9. Bishop Wilson T. Hogue, *Retrospect and Prospect: A Semi-Centennial Sermon Before the General Conference of the Free Methodist Church, in Chicago, Illinois, June 18, 1911* (Chicago: Free Methodist Publishing House, 1911), 28.

10. 2 Corinthians 1:18-19, NIV

11. G. K. Chesterton, "The Dragon at Hide and Seek," *Daylight and Nightmare: Uncollected Stories and Fables*, selected and arranged by Marie Smith (New York: Dodd, Mead, 1986), 93–99.

12. 2 Corinthians 6:16, NIV

13. I learned this phrase from William C. Taylor, *Practically Radical: Not-So-Crazy Ways to Transform Your Company, Shake Up Your Industry, and Challenge Yourself* (New York: William Morrow, 2011).

14. Abraham Cahan, *The Rise of David Levinsky* (Mineola, NY: Dover, 2002), 368.

CHAPTER 19: PLAY BALL!

1. *HalfTime*, premier issue (September/October 2002), 22.

2. Clay Shirky, *Cognitive Surplus: Creativity and Generosity in a Connected Age* (New York: Penguin, 2010).

3. Patrick Kavanagh, *Self Portrait* (Dublin: Dolmen Press, 1964). See also, http://www.ricorso.net/rx/library/authors/classic/Kavanagh_P/S_Portrait.htm.

CHAPTER 20: PLAY WITH FIRE
1. David J. Schlafer, *Playing with Fire: Preaching Work as Kindling Art* (Cambridge, MA: Cowley Publications, 2004).
2. Adin Steinsaltz, *On Being Free* (Northvale, NJ: Jason Aronson, 1995), 119–20.
3. William Morris, *A Dream of John Ball* [1888] (West Valley City, UT: Waking Lion Press, 2006), 21.

CONCLUSION: "YOU BRING ME GREAT PLEASURE!"
1. W. E. Sangster, *The Craft of Sermon Construction* [1949] (Grand Rapids, MI: Baker, 1972), 150.
2. Hebrews 10:38
3. Contra Joseph Campbell's famous saying in Joseph Campbell and Bill Moyers, *The Power of Myth* (New York: Anchor, 1991), 147ff.

Online Discussion *guide*

TAKE *your* TYNDALE READING EXPERIENCE *to the* NEXT LEVEL

A FREE discussion guide for this book is available at bookclubhub.net, perfect for sparking conversations in your book group or for digging deeper into the text on your own.

www.bookclubhub.net

You'll also find free discussion guides for other Tyndale books, e-newsletters, e-mail devotionals, virtual book tours, and more!

CP0071